PUBLISHED FOR THE MALONE SOCIETY BY
OXFORD UNIVERSITY PRESS

WALTON STREET, OXFORD OX2 6DP

Oxford   New York
Athens   Auckland   Bangkok   Bombay
Calcutta   Cape Town   Dar es Salaam   Delhi
Florence   Hong Kong   Istanbul   Karachi
Kuala Lumpur   Madras   Madrid   Melbourne
Mexico City   Nairobi   Paris   Singapore
Taipei   Tokyo   Toronto
and associated companies in
Berlin   Ibadan

ISBN 0 19 729033 7

Printed by BAS Printers Limited, Over Wallop, Hampshire

A MIDSUMMER
NIGHT'S DREAM
1600

THE MALONE SOCIETY
REPRINTS, VOL. 157
1995

This edition of *A Midsummer Night's Dream* (1600) was prepared by Thomas L. Berger and checked by G. R. Proudfoot and the General Editor.

The Society is grateful to the Huntington Library, California, for permission to reproduce its copy of the book (69334).

October 1995   ROGER HOLDSWORTH

INTRODUCTION

On 8 October 1600, the Stationers' *Register* records that Thomas Fisher paid vj^d to enter *A Midsummer Night's Dream*:

Tho. ffyffher   Entred for his copie vnder the | hande of m^r Rodes and the | Wardens. A booke called | A mydfõmer nighte dream[1]

Two early quarto editions of *A Midsummer Night's Dream* have survived, the first published in 1600, the second in 1619. The first edition, here reproduced in facsimile, was printed by Richard Bradock for Thomas Fisher, and is dated 1600. This quarto, signed 1–4, collates A–H^4. The title-page is A1^r; A1^v is blank. The text, with a head-title, commences on A2^r and concludes on H4^v. Most pages contain thirty-five lines of text, with the exception of D2^v and the first four pages of sheet G. D2^v, G1^r, G1^v, and G2^v contain thirty-four lines, while G2^r contains thirty-two lines.[2]

Eight copies of the quarto are known.[3] Collation of the eight copies reveals five press variants in four of the sixteen formes: the inner and outer formes

---

[1]   There is a facsimile of the Stationers' *Register* entry in S. Schoenbaum, *William Shakespeare: Records and Images* (London, 1981), p. 214, plate 116. Here and throughout the Introduction ʃ has been retained, but ligatures have been ignored. The quarto is listed in W. W. Greg, *A Bibliography of the English Printed Drama to the Restoration*, 4 vols. (London, 1939–59), i. 276–7 (No. 170). The 1600 quarto is STC 22302 (W. A. Jackson, F. S. Ferguson, and Katharine F. Pantzer, *A Short-Title Catalogue of Books Printed in England, Scotland, & Ireland, and of English Books Printed Abroad*, second edition, 3 vols. (London, 1976–91), ii. 326).

[2]   If he was setting by formes in sheet G, which seems unlikely, the compositor, for whatever reasons (illegible copy, revised copy, marginal additions), clearly miscast his copy. Even if he was setting seriatim in the two formes of sheet G, which seems more likely, there appear to have been some irregularities in the copy that produced the 'irregular' number of lines per page.

[3]   All the copies are listed, and their condition described, in Henrietta C. Bartlett and Alfred W. Pollard, *A Census of Shakespeare's Plays in Quarto: 1594–1700* (New Haven, 1939), pp. 70–1, hereafter abbreviated as B&P.

of sheet E, and the inner formes of sheets A and F.[4] The inner forme of sheet A exists in three states.

COPIES COLLATED

BL (British Library, C.34.k.29: B&P 743)
Bodl (Bodleian Library; C3 damaged: B&P 741)[5]
TCC (Trinity College Cambridge: B&P 748)
CSmH (Henry E. Huntington Library: B&P 747)
CtYEC (Yale Elizabethan Club: B&P 744)
DFo (Folger Shakespeare Library: B&P 745)
MB (Boston Public Library: B&P 742)
MH (Harvard University; lacks C2, C3, H2, H3: B&P 746)

---

[4] Often it is difficult to determine when a press variant exists, and the distinction between deliberate stop-press variants and accidental shifting and bad inking can be vexing to decide. Thus, the 'h' in 'both' at Q/TLN 137 (Sig. A3ᵛ) appears to have slipped slightly in the British Library copy, producing 'bot h', and the space between 'I' and 'know' at Q/TLN 1613 (Sig. F4ᵛ) is so loose that the Bodleian, Folger, Huntington, Harvard, and Yale Elizabethan Club copies read 'Iknow'. Similarly, 'O long' at Q/TLN 1440 (Sig. F2ʳ) has slipped significantly, producing 'Ol ong' in the British Library, Huntington, Yale Elizabethan Club, Folger, and Harvard copies. The hyphen in 'loue-ſhaft' at Q/TLN 527 (Sig. C1ʳ), clear in some copies, is so weakly inked as to appear almost invisible in the British Library, Trinity College Cambridge, and Yale Elizabethan Club copies. At Q/TLN 1124 (Sig. E1ᵛ) I agree with W. W. Greg that the Folger copy is variant and reads 'fwore' for 'ſwore'; but Richard F. Kennedy, textual editor of the New Variorum *Midsummer Night's Dream*, disagrees. Kennedy and I agree (*contra* Stanley Wells and Gary Taylor, *William Shakespeare: A Textual Companion* (Oxford, 1987), p. 287) that what appears to be a comma after 'melody' at Q/TLN 212 (Sig. A4ᵛ) in the Bodleian copy is an overinked full stop.

[5] Much of the bottom half of C3 has been torn off. It has been repaired with another piece of paper, and the missing quarto text added in a post seventeenth-century hand. The copyist placed a comma after an extant 'deere' at Q/TLN 685, which the Oxford editors mistook for a press variant (*Textual Companion*, pp. 281, 287).

PRESS VARIANTS[6]

SHEET A (*inner forme*)[7]

Corrected: BL, MH
Uncorrected: Bodl, TCC, CSmH, CtYEC, DFo, MB

Sig. A2ʳ, Q/TLN   17 Now] Now (turned initial 'N')

Corrected: BL, Bodl, TCC, CSmH, CtYEC, MB, MH
Uncorrected: DFo

Sig. A2ʳ, Q/TLN   31 to funerals:] ro funerals:

SHEET E (*outer forme*)

Corrected: BL, Bodl, TCC, CSmH, CtYEC, DFo, MH
Uncorrected: MB

Sig. E3ʳ, Q/TLN 1219 he] be

SHEET E (*inner forme*)

Corrected: BL, Bodl, TCC, CSmH, CtYEC, MB, MH
Uncorrected: DFo

Sig. E1ᵛ, Q/TLN 1124 ſwore] fwore

[6] Variants are identified by the signature in the Quarto, and their Q/TLN, with corrected states given first. From the estate of Charlton Hinman, Robert K. Turner, Jun., has provided me with the notes W. W. Greg compiled toward his projected facsimile of *A Midsummer Night's Dream*, Q1. For these I am appreciative, as I am for the many assistances, great and small, from Richard F. Kennedy.

[7] Given the shortage of extant copies, it is impossible to reconstruct with any certainty the printing of the inner forme of Sheet A.

First stage corrected: BL, Bodl, CSmH, CtYEC, DFo, MH
Uncorrected: TCC, MB

Sig. F1ᵛ, Q/TLN 1399 notwiſtanding] notwiſtandiug
                1401 them vp & down:] them vp & dowe:

*

Widespread agreement about textual matters in a number of relatively recent editions of *A Midsummer Night's Dream* and an oft-cited study of the 1600 quarto's composition and presswork make a detailed analysis of the quarto, its 1619 reprint, and the Folio version of 1623 unnecessary.[8] Rather, what is presented here is a summary of the major issues.

Thomas Fisher's career as a publisher and bookseller was a short one. He was freed as a draper on 8 November 1596 by Richard Smith and transferred to the Stationers' Company in 1600. Of the three other titles associated with him, Nicholas Breton's *Pasquil's Mistress* was printed in 1600, perhaps by Richard Bradock,[9] and John Marston's *Antonio and Mellida* and *Antonio's Revenge* were printed in 1602 by Bradock. In these last two Matthew Lownes appears to have had an interest as well, as his shop in St Dunstan's Church-yard is cited on the title-pages of both volumes.[10] Though Richard Bradock seems to have begun his career as a printer as early as 1581, it is not until 1598, six years after he married the widow of the printer Robert Robinson,[11] that the number of books identified with Bradock grows considerably. Among his products were several play texts: *The Conflict of Conscience*, 1581 (STC 25966–25966.5, Greg 78), *The Downfall of Robert, Earl of Huntington*, 1601 (STC 18271, Greg 179), *The Death of Robert, Earl of Huntington*, 1601 (STC 18269, Greg 180), *Antonio and Mellida*, 1602 (STC 17473, Greg 184), *Antonio's Revenge*, 1602 (STC 17474, Greg 185), *The Family of Love*, 1608

---

[8] Harold Brooks's Arden edition appeared in 1979, R. A. Foakes's New Cambridge edition in 1984, Stanley Wells and Gary Taylor's Oxford edition of Shakespeare's *Complete Works* in 1986–7, and Peter Holland's single-play Oxford edition in 1994. See R. K. Turner, Jun., 'Printing Methods and Textual Problems in *A Midsummer Night's Dream*, Q1', *Studies in Bibliography*, 15 (1962), 33–55.

[9] STC 3678; see STC, iii. 64, for information about Fisher.

[10] STC 17473, 17474.

[11] Edward Arber, ed., *A Transcript of the Registers of the Company of Stationers in London, 1554–1640 A.D.*, 5 vols. (London and Birmingham, 1875–94), iii. 702.

(STC 17879–17879a, Greg 263), *Humour Out of Breath*, 1608 (STC 6411, Greg 268), and *A Yorkshire Tragedy*, 1608 (STC 22340, Greg 272).

The copy that Fisher gave Bradock appears to have been Shakespeare's 'foul papers'. A number of 'Shakespearean' spellings (i.e., spellings which appear in the Hand D portion of *Sir Thomas More*) is evident in the quarto, most especially such double 'o' spellings as 'boorde' (Q/TLN 1768) 'dooe' (Q/TLN 229), 'hoord' (Q/TLN 1500), 'mooue' (Q/TLN 220, 299, 929), 'prooue' (Q/TLN 636, 1117, 1246, 1248, 2032), and 'ſhooes' (Q/TLN 1037), as well as such spellings as 'maruailes' (Q/TLN 803, 1490) and 'maruaile' (Q/TLN 740) (for 'marvellous' and 'marvel'). The stage directions (and lack thereof) give further evidence of authorial copy. Such general entries as '*Enter the Clownes*' (Q/TLN 801), '*Enter* Theſeus *and all his traine*' (Q/TLN 1571), and '*Enter* Quince, Flute, Thisby *and the rabble*' (Q/TLN 1691) are more authorial and imprecise than theatrical and specific. Authorial as well may be the lack of entries for Bottom (and Puck?) at Q/TLN 892, Lysander at Q/TLN 1418, and Flute/Thisby at Q/TLN 2041. Inconsistent names for characters may be another mark of foul papers. Both 'Puck' and 'Robin Goodfellow', 'Titania' and 'Queen of the Fairies', 'Oberon' and 'King of the Fairies', 'Theseus' and 'Duke', and 'Bottom' and 'Clown' are used in speech prefixes and stage directions; shortages of type may occasionally have caused such variation.

Using evidence from running titles and recurring type, R. K. Turner, Jun., contends that one compositor in Bradock's shop set type for the quarto. Beginning with sheet B, the compositor set the text by formes, one skeleton regularly imposing the inner formes and another skeleton the outer formes.[12] Turner's analysis of type shortages suggests some minor irregularities in composition, irregularities which seem to indicate that the compositor might well have been setting seriatim between one or two pages in certain sheets.[13]

---

[12] Turner, p. 34. Peter Blayney's observation that Turner's analysis needs to be considered in the light of Bradock's two (or three) presses casts some doubt on Turner's conclusions (see *The Texts of 'King Lear' and Their Origins* (Cambridge, 1982), pp. 91–3). But Bradock's having two (or three) presses does not mean that he need have employed more than one in the printing of the *Midsummer Night's Dream* quarto; indeed, the irregular lineation in the first four pages of sheet G suggests that the quarto was printed at one press.

[13] The first four pages of sheet G may be just such a case. See Turner, p. 39: 'Yet we must realize that when a compositor set a quarto by formes he did not necessarily have to set the type-pages in numerical sequence within the formes, although it is my distinct impression that this order was usually adopted. Nor did the compositor necessarily have to set either by formes or *seriatim*; he could, if he chose, combine the two methods.'

Of particular interest are the signs of Shakespeare's revisions that reveal themselves in the mislineations at the beginning of Act V. John Dover Wilson believed these revisions occurred over a long period of time,[14] but recent editors and commentators, working with Turner's bibliographical analysis, see the revisions as being already present in the foul papers, with the compositor struggling to fit revised copy, difficult if not impossible to cast off correctly, into the confines of the remaining thirteen pages of type. The following lines from the quarto may represent Shakespeare's revisions of and additions to his foul papers: Q/TLN 1741–3, 1747–52, 1765–8, 1770–2, 1794–6, 1802–6, and 1813–19.[15]

The second quarto of 1619 was set from the 1600 quarto.[16] Except for the first five pages of sheet G, it is a page-for-page reprint.[17] While the printer effected a number of corrections, he also introduced numerous errors. Q2, then, possesses no authority; its importance lies in the fact that the text of the First Folio was set from it.

The compositors of the First Folio text, though using the second quarto as copy,[18] clearly had another document to consult, by general consensus a playhouse promptbook of some sort. Most of the changes in the Folio have to do with stage directions. The Folio not only supplies Bottom's entry, missing in the quarto, at F/TLN 927 but specifies *with the Aſſe head*. When Bottom calls for 'the tongs and the bones' (Q/TLN 1496, F/TLN 1540), the Folio adds *Muſicke Tongs, Rurall Muſicke*. The stage direction in Act V, *Exit all but Wall* (F/TLN 1951), is added, but the quarto direction a few lines later, *Exit Lyon, Thysby, and Mooneſhine* (Q/TLN 1893, F/TLN 1955), now unnecessary, is retained. Perhaps the most notable Folio addition is at the end of Act III, where the stage direction reads *They ſleepe all the Act* (F/TLN 1507). This suggests that an act-division had been introduced here and so intimates that there might have been other act-divisions as well, leading to the conclusion that the playhouse manuscript consulted cannot

[14] New Shakespeare edition (Cambridge, 1924), pp. 80–6.
[15] See Appendix III of the Arden edition (pp. 163–4), the New Cambridge edition (pp. 136–8), and the single-play Oxford edition (pp. 257–65).
[16] The second quarto, '*Printed by Iames Roberts*, 1600', was in fact printed in 1619 with a false date by William Jaggard for the Shakespeare collection, known as the Pavier quartos, of that year. The 1619 quarto is STC 22303.
[17] These five pages rearrange the typography and spacing of Q1's G1ʳ–G2ᵛ and G3ʳ to effect more typographically pleasing and balanced pages.
[18] See Charlton Hinman, *The Printing and Proof-Reading of the First Folio of Shakespeare*, 2 vols. (Oxford, 1963), ii. 415–26.

have been compiled prior to 1609, when such divisions came into general use.[19] Also significant is the stage direction for the entry of the Mechanicals in Act V, '*Tawyer with a Trumpet before them*' (F/TLN 1924). The 'Tawyer' in question must be William Tawyer, who we know from the record of his burial in June 1625 was 'Mr. Heminges man'. When he became 'Mr. Heminges man' is unknown. What appears to be the case is that the prompt-book evolved over time, the '*They fleepe all the Act*' stage direction having been added, at the earliest, for a performance late in the first decade of the seventeenth century. Tawyer and his trumpet, however, could have been added at any time after the composition of the foul papers in the mid-1590s.

Another major change is the Folio's substitution of Egeus for Philostrate in Act V. It is impossible to determine just when this change was made. Egeus and Theseus' Lords replace Philostrate in the stage direction that opens Folio's *Actus Quintus* (Q/TLN 1736, F/TLN 1792), Theseus calls for Egeus rather than Philostrate (Q/TLN 1773, F/TLN 1833), and Egeus is given five speeches in the Folio that the quarto assigns to Philostrate (Q/TLN 1774, F/TLN 1834; Q/TLN 1778–9, F/TLN 1839–40; Q/TLN 1797–1806, F/TLN 1858–67; Q/TLN 1808–11, F/TLN 1869–72; and Q/TLN 1842, F/TLN 1903). Folio's catchword at O2^r (*Phil.*) and the speech prefix (*Phi.*) at the top of the next page (O2^v; F/TLN 1874) do not reflect the change to Egeus. Nor is it possible to determine when the change in Theseus' speech in the same scene, one in which he both reads and responds to the possible post-nuptial entertainments in the quarto (Q/TLN 1780–96) occurred. In the Folio the speech is divided between Theseus and Lysander, with Lysander reading the possible entertainments (F/TLN 1841–2, 1845–6, 1849–50, 1853–4) and Theseus responding (F/TLN 1843–4, 1847–8, 1851–2, 1855–7).[20]

[19] See Gary Taylor, 'The Structure of Performance: Act Intervals in the London Theatres, 1576–1642', in Gary Taylor and John Jowett, *Shakespeare Reshaped: 1606–1623* (Oxford, 1993), pp. 3–50.

[20] Peter Holland surveys the implications of these changes in his single-play Oxford edition, pp. 265–8, concluding that behind the alterations is Shakespeare's revising hand. See also Barbara Hodgdon, 'Gaining a Father: the Role of Egeus in the Quarto and the Folio', *Review of English Studies*, NS 37 (1986), 534–42. Following Capell, W. W. Greg, *The Shakespeare First Folio* (Oxford, 1955), pp. 243 ff., sees in the Egeus speech prefixes evidence that the actor playing Egeus doubled as Philostrate. Markings in the promptbook to that effect were taken as speech prefixes by the person who annotated the copy of Q2 that served as copy for the Folio; see the Arden edition, pp. xxxii–xxxiv.

The present reproduction of the first quarto is a 1:1 photofacsimile prepared from photographs of the Bridgewater copy in the Henry E. Huntington Library, San Marino, California.[21]

There are a few readings which, although decipherable in other copies, may be unclear in the photofacsimile of the Huntington–Bridgewater copy:

Q/TLN 628 of this,   Q/TLN 1443 thefe   Q/TLN 1454 My ... pafe with   Q/TLN 1455 will I reft mee, till   Q/TLN 1485 Giue   Q/TLN 1489 fcratch   Q/TLN 1649 Of   Q/TLN 2093 Fairies

*

This edition contains two forms of line reference:

1. In the inner margins are Through Line Numbers to the Quarto (Q/TLN), beginning with the title on A1ʳ. Catchwords are not included in the count.
2. In the outer margins are Through Line Numbers for the text of *A Midsummer Night's Dream* as it appears in the 1623 Folio (F/TLN) and is reproduced and numbered by Charlton Hinman in *The Norton Facsimile: The First Folio of Shakespeare*.[22]

[21] CSmH, B&P 747. This copy was acquired by the Egerton family before 1640, when it was catalogued by John Egerton, second Earl of Bridgewater. It was sold to Henry E. Huntington in March 1917 (see B&P, p. 70).

The Malone Society acknowledges with gratitude the permission given by the Henry E. Huntington Library to prepare this facsimile from the Bridgewater copy, the copy Greg had selected for his planned facsimile of the play. The Society is also grateful to the University of California Press, and to Kenneth Muir and Michael J. B. Allen, for the loan of the photographs of *A Midsummer Night's Dream* used in their *Shakespeare's Plays in Quarto* (Berkeley, 1981). The Society would also like to thank them retrospectively for the loan of the photographs of the quarto of *2 Henry IV* which helped to make possible the Society's facsimile of 1990.

[22] New York, 1968, pp. 163–80.

Hyphenated numbers are placed alongside single Quarto lines which contain something more than one Folio line (as with Q/TLN 74, which appears as two lines, F/TLN 61–2, in the Folio). A bracket indicates that two or more Quarto lines are printed as a single line in the Folio (as with Q/TLN 1863–4, which appears as F/TLN 1925 in the Folio).

Where the Quarto lacks something more than a word or phrase which appears in the Folio, the F/TLN of the last line before the omitted material is entered at the appropriate place, and is followed immediately by the F/TLN of the first line after it (for example, F/TLN 136 is followed by F/TLN 138 because at that point there is a line in the Folio which does not appear in the Quarto). Where the Quarto contains material which is not in the Folio, this is signalled by a plus sign, + (as with Q/TLN 2040–1, where 'he for a man; God warnd vs: | ſhe, for a woman; God bleſſe us.' is omitted in the Folio text).[23]

On pp. 65–6 below, there is a table of correspondences between the Quarto signatures, page numbers in the present edition, Quarto Through Line Numbers, and the act, scene, and line numbers which are given for *A Midsummer Night's Dream* in *The Riverside Shakespeare*.[24]

[23] Charlton Hinman introduced and explained this system in his Shakespeare Quarto Facsimiles of *Much Ado About Nothing* (Oxford, 1971), pp. x–xiii, and *Othello* (Oxford, 1975), pp. xii–xiv.

[24] Ed. G. Blakemore Evans (Boston, 1974), pp. 222–46. Marvin Spevack's *Complete and Systematic Concordance to the Works of Shakespeare*, vols. 1–6 (Hildesheim, 1968–70), is based on the Riverside text, as is his later *Harvard Concordance to Shakespeare* (Cambridge, Mass., 1973).

A
Midſommer nights
dreame.

As it hath beene ſundry times pub-
lickely acted, by the *Right* honoura-
ble, the Lord Chamberlaine his
ſeruants.

Written by William Shakeſpeare.

¶Imprinted at London, for *Thomas Fiſher*, and are to
be ſoulde at his ſhoppe, at the Signe of the White Hart,
in *Fleeteſtreete.* 1600.

A
MIDSOMMER NIGHTS
DREAME.

Enter Theseus, Hippolita, *with others.*

Theseus.

Ow faire *Hippolita*, our nuptiall hower
Draws on apaſe : ſower happy daies bring in
An other Moone: but oh,me thinks,how ſlow
This old Moone waues!She lingers my deſires,
Like to a Stepdame, or a dowager,
Long withering out a yong mans reuenewe.

Hɪp. Fower daies will quickly ſteepe themſelues in night:

Fower nights will quickly dreame away the time:
And then the Moone, like to a ſiluer bowe,
Now bent in heauen, ſhall beholde the night
Of our ſolemnities.

The. Goe *Philoſtrate*,
Stirre vp the *Athenian* youth to merriments,
Awake the peart and nimble ſpirit of mirth,
Turne melancholy foorth to funerals:
The pale companion is not for our pomp.

Hyppolita, I woo'd thee with my ſword,
And wonne thy loue, doing thee iniuries:
But I will wed thee in another key,
With pompe, with triumph, and with reueling.

Enter Egeus *and his daughter* Hermia, *and* Lyſander
and Helena, *and* Demetrius.

Ege. Happy be *Theſeus*,our renowned duke.
The. Thankes good *Egeus*. Whats the newes with thee?
Ege. Full of vexation,come I , with complaint

A2   A-

Againſt my childe, my daughter *Hermia*,
                    Stand forth Demetrius.
My noble Lord,
This man hath my conſent to marry her.
                    Stand forth Liſander.
And my gratious Duke,
This man hath bewitcht the boſome of my childe.
Thou, thou *Lyſander*, thou haſt giuen her rimes,
And interchang'd loue tokens with my childe:
Thou haſt, by moone-light, at her windowe ſung,
With faining voice, verſes of faining loue,
And ſtolne the impreſſion of her phantaſie:
With bracelets of thy haire, rings, gawdes, conceites,
Knackes, trifles, noſegaies, ſweete meates (meſſengers
Of ſtrong preuailement in vnhardened youth)
With cunning haſt thou filcht my daughters heart,
Turnd her obedience (which is due to mee)
To ſtubborne harſhneſſe . And, my gratious Duke,
Be it ſo, ſhe will not here, before your Grace,
Conſent to marry with *Demetrius*,
I beg the auncient priuiledge of *Athens*:
As ſhe is mine, I may diſpoſe of her:
Which ſhall be, either to this gentleman,
Or to her death; according to our lawe,
Immediatly prouided, in that caſe.

    The. What ſay you, *Hermia?* Be aduiſ'd, faire maid.
To you, your father ſhould be as a God:
One that compoſ'd your beauties : yea and one,
ro whome you are but as a forme in wax,
By him imprinted, and within his power,
To leaue the figure, or disfigure it:
Demetrius is a worthy gentleman.

    Her. So is *Liſander.*   *The.* In himſelfe he is:
But in this kinde, wanting your fathers voice,
The other muſt be held the worthier.

Her.

Her. I would my father lookt but with my eyes.

The. Rather your eyes must, with his iudgement, looke,

Her. I doe intreat your grace, to pardon mee,
I know not by what power, I am made bould,
Nor how it may concerne my modesty,
In such a presence, here to plead my thoughts:
But I beseech your Grace, that I may knowe
The worst that may befall mee in this case,
If I refuse to wed *Demetrius.*

The. Either to dy the death, or to abiure,
For euer, the society of men.
Therefore, faire *Hermia,* question your desires,
Knowe of your youth, examine well your blood,
Whether (if you yeelde not to your fathers choyce)
You can endure the liuery of a Nunne,
For aye to be in shady cloyster, mew'd
To liue a barraine sister all your life,
Chaunting faint hymnes, to the colde fruitlesse Moone,
Thrise blessed they, that master so there bloode,
To vndergoe such maiden pilgrimage:
But earthlyer happy is the rose distild,
Then that, which, withering on the virgin thorne,
Growes, liues, and dies, in single blessednesse.

Her. So will I growe, so liue, so die my Lord,
Ere I will yield my virgin Patent, vp
Vnto his Lordshippe, whose vnwished yoake
My soule consents not to giue souerainty.

The. Take time to pawse, and by the next newe moone,
The sealing day, betwixt my loue and mee,
For euerlasting bond of fellowshippe,
Vpon that day either prepare to dye,
For disobedience to your fathers will,
Or else to wed *Demetrius,* as he would,
Or on *Dianaes* altar to protest,
For aye, austeritie and single life.

A3

Deme.

5

Deme. Relent, sweete *Hermia,* and, *Lysander,* yeeld
Thy crazed title to my certaine right.

Lys. You haue her fathers loue, *Demetrius:*
Let me haue *Hermias:* doe you marry him.

Egeus. Scornefull *Lysander,* true, he hath my loue:
And what is mine, my loue shall render him.
And she is mine, and all my right of her
I doe estate vnto *Demetrius.*

Lysand. I am my Lord, as well deriu'd as hee,
As well possest : my loue is more than his:
My fortunes euery way as fairely rankt
(If not with vantage)as *Demetrius :*
And(which is more then all these boastes can be)
I am belou'd of beautious *Hermia.*
Why should not I then prosecute my right?
Demetrius, Ile auouch it to his heade,
Made loue to *Nedars* daughter, *Helena,*
And won her soule : and she(sweete Ladie)dotes,
Deuoutly dotes, dotes in Idolatry,
Vpon this spotted and inconstant man.

The. I must confesse, that I haue heard so much;
And, with *Demetrius,* thought to haue spoke thereof:
But, being ouer full of selfe affaires,
My minde did loose it, But *Demetrius* come,
And come *Egeus,* you shall goe with mee:
I haue some priuate schooling for you both.
For you, faire *Hermia,* looke you arme your selfe,
To fit your fancies, to your fathers will;
Or else, the Law of *Athens* yeelds you vp
(Which by no meanes we may extenuate)
To death, or to a vowe of single life.
Come my *Hyppolita* : what cheare my loue?
Demetrius and *Egeus* goe along:
I must employ you in some businesse,
Against our nuptiall, and conferre with you

Of

Of ſome thing, nerely that concernes your ſelues.

 Ege. With duety and deſire, we follow you,   *Exeunt.* 136

 Lyſand. How now my loue? Why is your cheeke ſo pale? 138

How chance the roſes there doe fade ſo faſt?

 Her. Belike, for want of raine: which I could well 140

Beteeme them, from the tempeſt of my eyes.

 Liſ. Eigh me: for aught that I could euer reade,

Could euer here by tale or hiſtory,

The courſe of true loue neuer did runne ſmoothe:

But either it was different in bloud;

 Her. O croſſe! too high to be inthrald to loue.

 Liſ. Or elſe miſgraffed, in reſpect of yeares;

 Her. O ſpight! too olde to be ingag'd to young.

 Liſ. Or elſe, it ſtoode vpon the choyce of friends;

 Her. O hell, to chooſe loue by anothers eyes!

 Lyſ. Or, if there were a ſympathy in choyce, 150

Warre, death or ſickneſſe, did lay ſrege to it;

Making it momentany, as a ſound;

Swift, as a ſhadowe; ſhort, as any dreame;

Briefe, as the lightning in the collied night,

That (in a ſpleene) vnfolds both heauen and earth;

And, ere a man hath power to ſay, beholde,

The iawes of darkeneſſe do deuoure it vp:

So quicke bright things come to confuſion.

 Her. If then true louers haue bin euer croſt, 160

It ſtands as an edict, in deſtiny:

Then let vs teach our triall patience:

Becauſe it is a cuſtomary croſſe,

As dewe to loue, as thoughts, and dreames, and ſighes,

Wiſhes; and teares; poore Fancies followers.

 Lyſ. A good perſwaſion: therefore heare mee, *Hermia:*

I haue a widowe aunt , a dowager, 170

Of great reuenew, and ſhe hath no childe:

From *Athens* is her houſe remote, ſeauen leagues:

And ſhe reſpectes mee, as her only ſonne:

         There.

    A4

There, gentle *Hermia*, may I marry thee:
And to that place, the sharpe *Athenian* law
Can not pursue vs. If thou louest mee, then
Steale forth thy fathers house, to morrow night:
And in the wood, a league without the towne
(Where I did meete thee once with *Helena*
To do obseruance to a morne of May)
There will I stay for thee.

   Her. My good *Lysander*,
I sweare to thee, by *Cupids* strongest bowe,
By his best arrowe, with the golden heade,
By the simplicitie of *Venus* doues,
By that which knitteth soules, and prospers loues,
And by that fire, which burnd the *Carthage* queene,
When the false *Troian* vnder saile was seene,
By all the vowes that euer men haue broke,
(In number more then euer women spoke)
In that same place thou hast appointed mee,
To morrow truely will I meete with thee.

   Lys. Keepe promise loue: looke, here comes *Helena*.

              Enter Helena.

   Her. God speede faire *Helena*: whither away?
   Hel. Call you mee faire? That faire againe vnsay.
Demetrius loues your faire: ò happy faire!
Your eyes are loadstarres, and your tongues sweete aire
More tunable then larke, to sheepeheards eare,
When wheat is greene, when hauthorne buddes appeare.
Sicknesse is catching: O, were fauour so,
Your words I catch, faire *Hermia*, ere I goe,
My eare should catch your voice, my eye, your eye,
My tongue should catch your tongues sweete melody.
Were the world mine, *Demetrius* being bated,
The rest ile giue to be to you translated.
O, teach mee how you looke, and with what Art,
You sway the motion of *Demetrius* heart.

                        I

Her. I frowne vpon him; yet hee loues mee ſtill.

Hel. O that your frowns would teach my ſmiles ſuch skil.

Her. I giue him curſes; yet he giues mee loue.

Hel. O that my prayers could ſuch affection mooue.

Her. The more I hate, the more he followes mee.

Hel. The more I loue, the more he hateth mee.

Her. His folly, *Helena*, is no fault of mine.

Hel. None but your beauty; would that fault were mine.

Her. Take comfort: he no more ſhall ſee my face:
Lyſander and my ſelfe will fly this place.
Before the time I did *Liſander* ſee,
Seem'd *Athens* as a Paradiſe to mee.
O then, what graces in my loue dooe dwell,
That hee hath turnd a heauen vnto a hell!

Lyſ. *Helen*, to you our mindes wee will vnfould:
To morrow night, when *Phœbe* doth beholde
Her ſiluer viſage, in the watry glaſſe,
Decking, with liquid pearle, the bladed graſſe
(A time, that louers flights doth ſtill conceale)
Through *Athens* gates, haue wee deuiſ'd to ſteale.

Her. And in the wood, where often you and I,
Vpon faint Primroſe beddes, were wont to lye,
Emptying our boſomes, of their counſell ſweld,
There my *Lyſander*, and my ſelfe ſhall meete,
And thence, from *Athens*, turne away our eyes,
To ſeeke new friends and ſtrange companions.
Farewell, ſweete playfellow: pray thou for vs,
And good lucke graunt thee thy *Demetrius*.
Keepe word *Lyſander*: we muſt ſtarue our ſight,
From louers foode, till morrow deepe midnight.

Exit Hermia.

Lyſ. I will my *Hermia*. *Helena* adieu:
As you on him, *Demetrius* dote on you. *Exit* Lyſander.

Hele. How happie ſome, ore otherſome, can be!
Through *Athens*, I am thought as faire as ſhee.

B   But

But what of that? *Demetrius* thinkes not so:
He will not knowe, what all, but hee doe know,
And as hee erres, doting on *Hermias* eyes:
So I, admiring of his qualities.
Things base and vile, holding no quantitie,
Loue can transpose to forme and dignitie.
Loue lookes not with the eyes, but with the minde:
And therefore is wingd *Cupid* painted blinde.
Nor hath loues minde of any iudgement taste:
Wings, and no eyes, figure, vnheedy haste.
And therefore is loue said to bee a childe:
Because, in choyce, he is so oft beguil'd.
As waggish boyes, in game, themselues forsweare:
So, the boy, Loue, is periur'd euery where.
For, ere *Demetrius* lookt on *Hermias* eyen,
Hee hayld downe othes, that he was onely mine,
And when this haile some heate, from *Hermia*, felt,
So he dissolued, and showrs of oathes did melt.
I will goe tell him of faire *Hermias* flight:
Then, to the wodde, will he, to morrow night,
Pursue her: and for this intelligence,
If I haue thankes, it is a deare expense:
But herein meane I to enrich my paine,
To haue his sight thither, and back againe.　　　*Exit.*

  Enter Quince, *the Carpenter; and* Snugge, *the Ioyner; and*
  Bottom, *the Weauer; and* Flute, *the Bellowes mender; &*
  Snout, *the Tinker; and* Starueling *the Tayler.*
  Qnin. Is all our company heere?
  Bot. You were best to call them generally, man by
man, according to the scrippe.
  Quin. Here is the scrowle of euery mans name, which is
thought fit, through al *Athens*, to play in our Enterlude, be-
fore the Duke, & the Dutches, on his wedding day at night.
  Bott. First good *Peeter Quince*, say what the Play treats on:
then read the names of the Actors: & so grow to a point.
                   Quin.

250   260

260   270

270   280

Quin. Mary, our Play is the moſt lamentable comedy, and moſt cruell death of *Pyramus* and *Thiſby.* 280

Bot. A very good peece of worke, I aſſure you, & a merry. Now good *Peeter Quince,* call forth your Actors, by the ſcrowle. Maſters, ſpreade your ſelues. 290

Quin. Anſwere, as I call you. *Nick Bottom,* the Weauer?

Bott. Readie : Name what part I am for, and proceede.

Quin. You, *Nick Bottom* are ſet downe for *Pyramus.*

Bott. What is *Pyramus?* A louer, or a tyrant? 290

Quin. A louer that kils himſelfe, moſt gallant, for loue.

Bott. That will aſke ſome teares in the true performing of it. If I doe it, let the Audience looke to their eyes: I wil mooue ſtormes : I will condole, in ſome meaſure. To the reſt yet, my chieſe humour is for a tyrant. I could play *Er-* 300 *cles* rarely, or a part to teare a Cat in , to make all ſplit the raging rocks : and ſhiuering ſhocks, ſhall breake the locks of priſon gates, and *Phibbus* carre ſhall ſhine from farre, and make & marre the fooliſh Fates. This was loſtie. Now, 300–1 name the reſt of the Players. This is *Ercles* vaine, a tyrants vaine : A louer is more condoling.

Quin. Francis Flute, the Bellowes mender?

Flu. Here *Peeter Quince.*

Quin. Flute, you muſt take *Thiſby,* on you.

Fla. What is *Thiſby?* A wandring knight? 310

Quin. It is the Lady, that *Pyramus* muſt loue. (ming.

Fl. Nay faith: let not me play a womā: I haue a beard cō- 310

Quin. Thats all one: you ſhall play it in a Maſke: and you may ſpeake as ſmall as you will.

Bott. And I may hide my face, let me play *Thiſby* to : Ile ſpeake in a monſtrous little voice; *Thiſne, Thiſne,* ah *Py-ramus,* my louer deare, thy *Thyſby* deare, & Lady deare. 317–18

Qu. No, no: you muſt play *Pyramus:* & *Flute,* you *Thyſby.* 319–20

Bot. Well, proceede. *Qui. Robin Starueling,* the Tailer?

Star. Here *Peeter Quince.* 322–3

Quin. Robin Starueling, you muſt play *Thyſbyes* mother:

B2 Tom

Tom Snowte, the Tinker?

Snowt. Here *Peter Quince*.

Quin. You, *Pyramus* father; my selfe, *Thisbies* father; *Snugge*, the Ioyner, you the Lyons part : And I hope here is a Play fitted.

Snug. Haue you the Lyons part written? Pray you, if it bee, giue it meet for I am slowe of studie.

Quin. You may doe it, *extempore*: for it is nothing but roaring.

Bott. Let mee play the Lyon to. I will roare, that I will doe any mans heart good to heate mee. I will roare, that I will make the Duke say; Let him roare againe : let him roare againe.

Quin. And you should do it too terribly, you would fright the Dutchesse, and the Ladies, that they would shrike : and that were inough to hang vs all.

All. That would hang vs, euery mothers sonne.

Bot. I grant you, friends, if you should fright the Ladies out of their wits, they would haue no more discretion, but to hang vs: but I will aggrauate my voice so, that I wil roare you as gently, as any sucking doue : I will roare you, and 'twere any Nightingale.

Quin. You can play no part but *Piramus*: for *Piramus* is a sweete fac't man; a proper man as one shall see in a sommers day; a most louely gentlemanlike man : therefore you must needes play *Piramus*:

Bot. Well: I will vndertake it. What beard were I best to play it in?

Quin. Why? what you will.

Bot. I wil discharge it, in either your straw colour beard, your Orange tawnie bearde, your purple in graine beard, or your french crowne colour beard, your perfit yellow.

Quin. Some of your french crownes haue no haire at all; and then you will play bare fac't. But maisters here are your parts, and I am to intreat you, request you, and desire you

you, to con them by to morrow night : and meete mee in
the palace wood, a mile without the towne, by Moone-
light; there will wee rehearse : for if wee meete in the city,
wee shal be dogd with company, and our deuises known.
In the meane time, I will draw a bill of properties, such as
our play wants. I pray you faile me not.

Bot. Wee will meete, & there we may rehearse most ob-
scenely, and coragiously. Take paines, bee perfit : adieu.

Quin. At the Dukes oke wee meete.

Bot. Enough: holde, or cut bowstrings.   *Exeunt.*

    ¶ *Enter a* Fairie *at one doore, and* Robin goodfellow
                  at another.

    Robin. How now spirit, whither wander you?

    Fa. Ouer hill, ouer dale, thorough bush, thorough brier,
Ouer parke, ouer pale, thorough flood, thorough fire:
I do wander euery where; swifter than the Moons sphere:
And I serue the Fairy Queene, to dew her orbs vpon the
The cowslippes tall her Pensioners bee,   (greene.
In their gold coats, spottes you see:
Those be Rubies, Fairie fauours:
In those freckles, liue their sauours.
I must goe seeke some dew droppes here,
And hang a pearle in euery cowslippes eare.
Farewell thou Lobbe of spirits: Ile be gon.
Our Queene, and all her Elues come here anon.

    Rob. The king doth keepe his Reuels here to night.
Take heede the Queene come not within his sight.
For *Oberon* is passing fell and wrath:
Because that shee, as her attendant, hath
A louely boy stollen, from an Indian king:
She neuer had so sweete a changeling.
And iealous *Oberon* would haue the childe,
Knight of his traine, to trace the forrests wilde.
But shee, perforce, withhoulds the loued boy,
Crownes him with flowers, and makes him all her ioy.   And

B 3

And now, they neuer meete in groue, or greene,
By fountaine cleare, or spangled starlight sheene,
But they doe square, that all their Elues, for feare,
Creepe into acorne cups, and hide them there.

Fa. Either I mistake your shape, and making, quite,
Or els you are that shrewde and knauish sprite,
Call'd *Robin goodfellow*. Are not you hee,
That frights the maidens of the Villageree,
Skim milke, and sometimes labour in the querne,
And bootlesse make the breathlesse huswife cherne,
And sometime make the drinke to beare no barme,
Misselead nightwanderers, laughing at their harme?
Those, that Hobgoblin call you, and sweete Puck,
You doe their worke, and they shall haue good luck.
Are not you hee?

Rob. Thou speakest aright; I am that merry wanderer of
I ieast to *Oberon*, and make him smile, (the night,
When I a fat and beane-fed horse beguile;
Neyghing, in likenesse of a filly fole,
And sometime lurke I in a gossippes bole,
In very likenesse of a rosted crabbe,
And when she drinkes, against her lips I bob,
And on her withered dewlop, poure the ale.
The wisest aunt, telling the saddest tale,
Sometime, for three foote stoole, mistaketh mee:
Then slippe I from her bumme, downe topples she,
And tailour cryes, and falles into a coffe;
And then the whole Quire hould their hippes, and lofte,
And waxen in their myrth, and neeze, and sweare
A merrier hower was neuer wasted there.
But roome Faery: here comes *Oberon*.

Fa. And here, my mistresse. Would that he were gon.

Enter the King of Fairies, at one doore, with his traine, and the Queene, at another, with hers.

Ob. Ill met by moonelight, proud *Tytania*.

Qu.

14

Qu. What, Iealous *Oberon?* Fairy skippe hence.
I haue forsworne his bedde, and company.

Ob. Tarry, rash wanton. Am not I thy Lord?

Qu. Then I must be thy Lady: but I know
When thou hast stollen away from Fairy land,
And in the shape of *Corin*, sat all day,
Playing on pipes of corne, and versing loue,
To amorous *Phillida*, Why art thou here
Come from the farthest steppe of *India?*
But that, forsooth, the bounsing *Amason*,
Your buskind mistresse, and your warriour loue,
To *Theseus* must be wedded; and you come,
To giue their bedde, ioy and prosperitie.

Ob. How canst thou thus, for shame, *Tytania*,
Glaunce at my credit, with *Hippolita?*
Knowing, I know thy loue to *Theseus*,
Didst not thou lead him through the glimmering night,
From *Perigenia*, whom he rauished?
And make him, with faire Eagles, breake his faith
With *Ariadne*, and *Antiopa?*

Quee. These are the forgeries of iealousie:
And neuer, since the middle Sommers spring,
Met we on hill, in dale, forrest, or meade,
By paued fountaine, or by rushie brooke,
Or in the beached margent of the Sea,
To daunce our ringlets to the whistling winde,
But with thy brawles thou hast disturbd our sport.
Therefore the windes, pyping to vs in vaine,
As in reuenge, haue suckt vp, from the Sea,
Contagious fogges: which, falling in the land,
Hath euery pelting riuer made so proude,
That they haue ouerborne their Continents,
The Oxe hath therefore stretcht his yoake in vaine,
The Ploughman lost his sweat, and the greene corne
Hath rotted, ere his youth attainde a bearde:

B4　　　　　　The

The fold ſtands empty, in the drowned field,
And crowes are fatted with the murrion flocke.
The nine mens Morris is fild vp with mudde:
And the queint Mazes, in the wanton greene,
For lacke of tread, are vndiſtinguiſhable.
The humane mortals want their winter heere.
No night is now with hymne or carroll bleſt.
Therefore the Moone (the gouerneſſe of floods) 470
Pale in her anger, waſhes all the aire;
That Rheumaticke diſeaſes doe abound. 480
And, thorough this diſtemperature, wee ſee
The ſeaſons alter: hoary headed froſts
Fall in the freſh lappe of the Crymſon roſe,
And on old *Hyems* chinne and Icy crowne,
An odorous Chaplet of ſweete Sommer buddes
Is, as in mockery, ſet. The Spring, the Sommer,
The childing Autumne, angry Winter change
Their wonted Liueries: and the mazed worlde,
By their increaſe, now knowes not which is which? 480
And this ſame progeny of euils, 490
Comes from our debate, from our diſſention:
We are their Parents and originall.
   Oberon. Doe you amend it then? it lyes in you.
Why ſhould *Titania* croſſe her *Oberon*?
I doe but begge a little Changeling boy,
To be my Henchman.
   Queene. Set your heart at reſt.
The Faiery Land buies not the childe of mee. 490
His mother was a Votreſſe of my order: 500
And in the ſpiced *Indian* ayer, by night,
Full often hath ſhe goſſipt, by my ſide,
And ſat, with me on *Neptunes* yellow ſands
Marking th'embarked traders on the flood?
When we haue laught to ſee the ſailes conceaue,
And grow bigge bellied, with the wanton winde:

                               Which

Which she, with prettie, and with swimming gate,
Following (her wombe then rich with my young squire)
Would imitate, and saile vpon the land,
To fetch me trifles, and returne againe,
As from a voyage, rich with marchandise.
But she, being mortall, of that boy did dye,
And, for her sake, doe I reare vp her boy:
And, for her sake, I will not part with him.

   Ob. How long, within this wood, entend you stay?

   Quee. Perchaunce, till after *Theseus* wedding day.
If you will patiently daunce in our Round,
And see our Moonelight Reuelles, goe with vs:
If not, shunne me, and I will spare your haunts,

   Ob. Giue mee that boy, and I will goe with thee.

   Quee. Not for thy Fairy kingdome. Fairies away.
We shall chide downeright, if I longer stay.   *Exeunt.*

   Ob. Well: goe thy way. Thou shalt not from this groue,
Till I torment thee, for this iniury.
My gentle *Pucke* come hither: thou remembrest,
Since once I sat vpon a promontory,
And heard a Mearemaide, on a Dolphins backe,
Vttering such dulcet and hermonious breath,
That the rude sea grewe ciuill at her song,
And certaine starres shot madly from their Spheares,
To heare the Sea-maids musicke,

   Puck. I remember,

   Ob. That very time, I saw (but thou could'st not)
Flying betweene the colde Moone and the earth,
Cupid, all arm'd: a certaine aime he tooke
At a faire Vestall, throned by west,
And loos'd his loue-shaft smartly, from his bowe,
As it should pearce a hundred thousand hearts:
But, I might see young *Cupids* fiery shaft
Quencht in the chast beames of the watry Moone:
And the imperiall Votresse passed on,
      C   In

In maiden meditation, fancy free.
Yet markt I, where the bolt of *Cupid* fell.
It fell vpon a little wetterne flower;
Before, milke white; now purple, with loues wound,
And maidens call it, Loue in idlenesse.
Fetch mee that flowre : the herbe I shewed thee once.
The iewce of it, on sleeping eyeliddes laide,
Will make or man or woman madly dote,
Vpon the next liue creature that it sees.
Fetch mee this herbe, and be thou here againe
Ere the *Leuiathan* can swimme a league.
Pu. Ile put a girdle, roûd about the earth, in forty minutes.
  Oberon. Hauing once this iuice,
Ile watch *Titania*, when she is a sleepe,
And droppe the liquor of it, in her eyes:
The next thing then she, waking, lookes vpon
(Be it on Lyon, Beare, or Wolfe, or Bull,
On medling Monky, or on busie Ape)
She shall pursue it, with the soule of Loue.
And ere I take this charme, from of her sight
(As I can take it with another herbe)
Ile make her render vp her Page, to mee.
But, who comes here? I am inuisible,
And I will ouerheare their conference.
    Enter Demetrius, Helena *following him.*
  Deme. I loue thee not: therefore pursue me not,
Where is *Lysander*, and faire *Hermia?*
The one Ile stay: the other stayeth me.
Thou toldst me, they were stolne vnto this wood:
And here am I, and wodde, within this wood:
Because I cannot meete my *Hermia.*
Hence, get the gone, and follow mee no more.
  Hel. You draw mee, you hard hearted Adamant:
But yet you draw not Iron. For my heart
Is true as steele. Leaue you your power to draw,

                        And

And I shall haue no power to follow you.

  Deme. Doe I entise you? Doe I speake you faire?
Or rather doe I not in plainest truthe,
Tell you I doe not, not I cannot loue you?

  Hele. And euen, for that, do I loue you, the more:
I am your Spaniell: and, *Demetrius,*
The more you beat mee, I will fawne on you.
Vse me but as your Spaniell: spurne me, strike mee,
Neglect mee, loose me: onely giue me leaue
(Vnworthie as I am) to follow you.
What worser place can I begge, in your loue
(And yet, a place of high respect with mee)
Then to be vsed as you vse your dogge.

  Deme. Tempt not, too much, the hatred of my spirit.
For I am sick, when I do looke on thee.

  Hele. And I am sick, when I looke not on you.

  Deme. You doe impeach your modestie too much,
To leaue the citie, and commit your selfe,
Into the hands of one that loues you not,
To trust the opportunitie of night,
And the ill counsell of a desert place,
With the rich worth of your virginitie.

  Hel. Your vertue is my priuiledge: For that
It is not night, when I doe see your face.
Therefore, I thinke, I am not in the night,
Nor doth this wood lacke worlds of company.
For you, in my respect, are all the world.
Then, how can it be saide, I am alone,
When all the world is here, to looke on mee?

  Deme. Ile runne from thee, and hide me in the brakes,
And leaue thee to the mercy of wilde beastes.

  Hel. The wildest hath not such a heart as you.
Runne when you will: The story shall be chaung'd:
Apollo flies and *Daphne* holds the chase:
The Doue pursues the Griffon: the milde Hinde

C 2   Makes

Makes ſpeede to catch the Tigre. Booteleſſe ſpeede,
When cowardiſe purſues, and valour flies.

   Demet. I will not ſtay thy queſtions, Let me goe:
Or if thou followe mee, do not beleeue,
But I ſhall doe thee miſchiefe, in the wood.

   Hel. I, in the Temple, in the towne, the fielde,
You doe me miſchiefe. Fy *Demetrius.*
Your wrongs doe ſet a ſcandall on my ſex:
We cannot fight for loue , as men may doe:
We ſhould be woo'd, and were not made to wooe.
Ile follow thee and make a heauen of hell,
To dy vpon the hand I loue ſo well.

   Ob. Fare thee well Nymph. Ere he do leaue this groue,
Thou ſhalt fly him, and he ſhall ſeeke thy loue.
Haſt thou the flower there? Welcome wanderer.

              Enter Pucke.

   Puck. I, there it is.

   Ob. I pray thee giue it mee.
I know a banke where the wilde time blowes,
Where Oxlips, and the nodding Violet growes,
Quite ouercanopi'd with luſhious woodbine,
With ſweete muſke roſes, and with Eglantine:
There ſleepes *Tytania*, ſometime of the night,
Luld in theſe flowers, with daunces and delight:
And there the ſnake throwes her enammeld ſkinne,
Weed wide enough to wrappe a Fairy in.
And, with the iuyce of this, Ile ſtreake her eyes,
And make her full of hatefull phantaſies.
Take thou ſome of it, and ſeeke through this groue:
A ſweete *Athenian* Lady is in loue,
With a diſdainefull youth : annoint his eyes.
But doe it, when the next thing he eſpies,
May be the Ladie. Thou ſhalt know the man,
By the *Athenian* garments he hath on.
Effect it with ſome care; that he may prooue

                            More

More fond on her, then she vpon her loue:
And looke thou meete me ere the first Cocke crowe.

Pu. Feare not my Lord: your seruant shall do so. *Exeunt.*

Enter Tytania *Queene of Fairies, with her traine.*

Quee. Come, now a Roundell, and a Fairy song:
Then, for the third part of a minute hence,
Some to kill cankers in the musk rose buds,
Some warre with Reremise, for their lethren wings,
To make my small Elues coates, and some keepe backe
The clamorous Owle, that nightly hootes and wonders
At our queint spirits : Sing me now a sleepe:
Then to your offices, and let mee rest.

Fairies sing.

You spotted Snakes, with double tongue,
Thorny Hedgehogges be not seene,
Newts and blinde wormes do no wrong,
Come not neere our Fairy Queene.
Philomele, with melody,
Sing in our sweete Lullaby,
Lulla, lulla, lullaby, lulla, lulla, lullaby,
Neuer harme, nor spell, nor charme,
Come our louely lady nigh.
So good night, with lullaby.

1, *Fai.* Weauing Spiders come not heere,
Hence you long legd Spinners, hence:
Beetles blacke approach not neere:
Worme nor snaile doe no offence.
Philomele with melody, &c.

2, *Fai.* Hence away : now all is well,
One aloofe, stand Centinell.

Enter Oberon.

Ob. What thou seest, when thou doest wake,
Doe it for thy true loue take:
Loue and languish for his sake.
Be it Ounce, or Catte, or Beare,

C 3   Pard,

Pard, or Boare with briſtled haire,
In thy eye that ſhall appeare,
When thou wak'ſt, it is thy deare:
Wake, when ſome vile thing is neere.

     Enter Lyſander: *and* Hermia.

 Lyſ. Faire loue, you fainte, with wandring in the woods
And to ſpeake troth I haue forgot our way.
Weele reſt vs *Hermia*, if you thinke it good,
And tarry for the comfor of the day.

 Her. Bet it ſo *Lyſander* : finde you out a beddes
For I, vpon this banke, will reſt my head.

 Lyſ. One turſe ſhall ſerue, as pillow, for vs both,
One heart, one bedde, two boſomes, and one troth.

 Her. Nay god *Lyſander* : for my ſake, my deere
Ly ſurther off, yet ; doe not lye ſo neere.

 Lyſ. O take the ſenſe, ſweete, of my innocence.
Loue takes the meaning, in loues conference,
I meane that my heart vnto yours it knit;
So that but one heart wee can make of it:
Two boſomes interchained with an oath:
So then two boſomes, and a ſingle troth.
Then, by your ſide, no bed-roome me deny:
For lying ſo, *Hermia*, I doe not lye.

 Her. Lyſander riddles very prettily.
Now much beſhrewe my manners, and my pride,
If *Hermia* meant to ſay, *Lyſander* lyed.
But gentle friend, for loue and curteſie,
Ly further off, in humane modeſly:
Such ſeparation, as may well be ſaid
Becomes a vertuous batcheler, and a maide,
So farre be diſtant, and good night ſweete friend:
Thy loue nere alter till thy ſweete life end.

 Lyſ. Amen, amen, to that faire prayer, ſay I,
And then end life, when I end loyalty.
Heere is my bed: ſleepe giue thee all his reſt.

           VVith

690

680

700

690

710

700

Her. With halfe that wiſh, the wiſhers eyes be preſt,

Enter Pucke.   718

Puck. Through the forreſt haue I gone:

But *Athenian* found I none,   720

On whoſe eyes I might approue

This flowers force in ſtirring loue.

Night and ſilence .Who is heere?

Weedes of *Athens* he doth weare:

This is hee (my maſter ſaide)

Deſpiſed the *Athenian* maide:

And here the maiden, ſleeping ſound,

On the danke and dirty ground.

Pretty ſowle, ſhe durſt not lye,   730

Neere this lack-loue, this kil-curteſie.

Churle , vpon thy eyes I throwe

All the power this charme doth owe:

When thou wak'ſt, let loue forbidde

Sleepe, his ſeat, on thy eye lidde.

So awake, when I am gon:

For I muſt now to *Oberon*.   *Exit.*

Enter Demetrius *and* Helena *running.*

Hel. Stay; though thou kill mee, ſweete *Demetrius.*

De. I charge thee hence, and doe not haunt mee thus

Hele. O, wilt thou darkling leaue me? doe not ſo.   740

De. Stay, on thy perill : I alone will goe.   741

Hel. O, I am out of breath, in this fond chaſe,   743

The more my prayer, the leſſer is my grace.

Happie is *Hermia*, whereſoere ſhe lies:

For ſhe hath bleſſed, and attractiue eyes.

How came her eyes ſo bright? Not with ſalt teares,

If ſo, my eyes are oftner waſht then hers.

No, no : I am as vgly as a Beare: 750

For beaſtes that meete mee, runne away, for feare.

Therefore, no maruaile, though *Demetrius*

Doe, as a monſter, fly my preſence, thus.

C 4   What

What wicked and diſſembling glaſſe, of mine,
Made me compare with *Hermia* ſphery eyen!
But, who is here? *Lyſander*, on the ground?
Dead, or a ſleepe? I ſee no blood, no wound,
Lyſander, if you liue, good ſir awake.

 Lyſ. And runne through fire, I will for thy ſweete ſake.
Tranſparent *Helena*, nature ſhewes arte,
That through thy boſome, makes me ſee thy heart.
Where is *Demetrius?* Oh how fit a word
Is that vile name, to periſh on my ſworde!

 Hel. Do not ſay ſo, *Lyſander*, ſay not ſo.
What though he loue your *Hermia?* Lord, what though?
Yet *Hermia* ſtill loues you : then be content.

 Lyſ. Content with *Hermia?* No : I doe repent
The tedious minutes, I with her haue ſpent.
Not *Hermia*, but *Helena* I loue.
VVho will not change a Rauen for a doue?
The will of man is by his reaſon ſwai'd:
And reaſon ſaies you are the worthier maide.
Things growing are not ripe, vntill their ſeaſon:
So I, being young, till now ripe not to reaſon.
And touching now, the point of humane skill,
Reaſon becomes the Marſhall to my will,
And leads mee to your eyes; where I orelooke
Loues ſtories, written in loues richeſt booke.

 Hel. Wherefore was I to this keene mockery borne?
When, at your hands, did I deſerue this ſcorne?
Iſt not enough, iſt not enough, young man,
That I did neuer, no nor neuer can,
Deſerue a ſweete looke from *Demetrius* eye,
But you muſt flout my inſufficiency?
Good troth you doe mee wrong(good ſooth you doe)
In ſuch diſdainfull manner, mee to wooe.
But, fare you well : perſorce, I muſt conſeſſe,
I thought you Lord of more true gentleneſſe.

             O₃

O, that a Ladie, of one man refus'd ,
Should, of another, therefore be abus'd!   *Exit.*

  Lyf. She sees not *Hermia* . *Hermia*, sleepe thou there,
And neuer maist thou come *Lyfander* neere.
For, as a surfet of the sweetest things
The deepest loathing, to the stomacke bringes:
Or, as the heresies, that men doe leaue,
Are hated most of those they did deceiue:
So thou, my surfet, and my heresie,
Of all bee hated; but the most, of mee:
And all my powers addresse your loue and might,
To honour *Helen*, and to be her knight.   *Exit.*

  Her. Helpe mee *Lyfander*, helpe mee : do thy best
To pluck this crawling serpent, from my brest.
Ay mee, for pittie. What a dreame was here?
Lyfander looke, how I doe quake with feare.
Me thoughr, a serpent eate my heart away,
And you sate smiling at his cruell pray.
Lyfander what, remou'd? *Lyfander*, Lord,
What, out of hearing, gon? No sound, no word?
Alacke where are you? Speake, and if you heare:
Speake, of all loues. I swoune almost with feare.
No, then I well perceiue, you are not ny:
Either death, or you, Ile finde immediately.   *Exit.*

Enter the Clownes.

  Bott. Are wee all met?

  Quin. Pat, pat : and heres a maruailes conuenient place,
for our rehearsall. This greene plot shall be our stage, this
hauthorne brake our tyring house, and wee will doe it in
action, as wee will doe it before the Duke.

  Bott. Peeter Quince?

  Qnin. What saiest thou, bully, *Bottom?*

  Bot. There are things in this Comedy , of *Pyramus* and
Thifby, that will neuer please. First, *Pyramus* must draw
a sworde, to kill himselfe; which the Ladies cannot abide.

D   How

How anſwere you that?

Snout. Berlakin, a parlous feare.

Star. I beleeue, we muſt leaue the killing, out, when all is done.

Bott. Not a whit : I haue a deuiſe to make all well. Write me a Prologue, and let the Prologue ſeeme to ſay; we wil do no harme, with our ſwords, and that *Pyramus* is not kild indeede : and for the more better aſſurance, tel them, that I *Pyramus* am not *Pyramus*, but *Bottom* the weauer: this will put them out of feare.

Quin. Well: wee will haue ſuch a Prologue, and it ſhall be written in eight and ſix.

Bot. No : make it two more : let it be written in eight & eight.

Snout. Will not the ladies be afeard of the Lyon?

Star. I feare it, I promiſe you.

Bot. Maſters, you ought to conſider with your ſelfe, to bring in (God ſhielde vs) a Lyon among Ladies, is a moſt dreadfull thing. For there is not a more fearefull wilde foule then your Lyon liuing : & we ought to looke toote.

Sno. Therfore, another Prologue muſt tel, he is not a Lion.

Bot. Nay : you muſt name his name, and halfe his face muſt be ſeene through the Lions necke, and he himſelſe muſt ſpeake through, ſaying thus, or to the ſame defeƈt; Ladies, or faire Ladies, I would wiſh you, or I would requeſt you, or I wold intreat you, not to feare, not to treble: my life for yours. If you thinke I come hither as a Lyon, it were pittie of my life. No : I am no ſuch thing : I am a man as other men are : & there indeed, let him name his name, and tell them plainely he is *Snugge*, the Ioyner.

Quin. Well: it ſhall be ſo : but there is two hard things; that is, to bring the Moone-light into a chamber : for you know, *Pyramus* and *Thiſby* meete by Moone-light.

Sn. Doth the Moone ſhine, that night, we play our Play?

Bot,

Bo. A Calender, a Calender: looke in the Almanack: finde out Moone-shine, finde out Moone-shine. 864

Quin. Yes: it doth shine that night. 866

Cet. Why then, may you leaue a casement of the great chamber window (where we play) open; and the Moone may shine in at the casement. 850

Quin. 1: or els, one must come in, with a bush of thorns, 870
& a latern, and say he comes to disfigure, or to present the person of Moone-shine. Then, there is another thing; we must haue a wal in the great chāber: for *Pyramus* & *Thisby* (saies the story) did talke through the chinke of a wall.

Sno. You can neuer bring in a wal. What say you *Bottom*? 876-7

Bot. Some man or other must present wall: and let him haue some plaster, or som lome, or some rough cast, about 880
him, to signifie wall; or let him holde his fingers thus: and 860
through that crany, shall *Pyramus* and *Thisby* whisper.

Quin. If that may be, then all is well. Come, sit downe euery mothers sonne, and reherse your parts. *Pyramus*, you beginne: when you haue spoken yonr speech, enter into that Brake, and so euery one according to his cue.

Enter Robin.

Ro. What hempen homespunnes haue we swaggring here, 889-90
So neere the Cradle of the Fairy Queene? 870
What, a play toward? Ile be an Auditor,
An Actor to perhappes, If I see cause.

Quin. Speake *Pyramus*: *Thysby* stand forth.

Pyra. *Thisby* the flowers of odious sauours sweete.

Quin. Odours, odorous.

Py. Odours sauours sweete.
So hath thy breath, my dearest *Thisby* deare.
But harke, a voice: stay thou but heere a while,
And by and by I will to thee appeare. *Exit.* 900

Quin. A stranger *Pyramus*, then ere played heere. 880

Thys. Must I speake now?

D.2　　　　　　　　　　　　　　　　I

Quin. I marry muſt you. For you muſt vnderſtãd, he goes but to ſee a noyſe, that he heard, and is to come againe.

Thyſ. Moſt radiant *Pyramus*, moſt lillie white of hewe,
Of colour like the redroſe, on triumphant bryer,
Moſt brisky Iunenall, and eeke moſt louely Iewe,
As true as trueſt horſe, that yet would neuer tyre,
Ile meete thee *Pyramus*, at *Ninnies* toumbe.

Quin. Ninus toumbe, man. Why? you muſt not ſpeake
That yet. That you anſwere to *Pyramus*. You ſpeake
Al your part at once, cues, and, all. *Pyramus*, enter: your cue
is paſt : It is; neuer tire.

Thyſ. O, as true as trueſt horſe, that yet would neuer tyre.

Py. If I were faire, *Thyſby*, I were onely thine.

Quin. O monſtrous! O ſtrange! We are haunted. Pray maſters: fly maſters: helpe.

Rob. Ile follow you: Ile leade you about a Round,
Through bogge, through buſh, through brake, through
Sometime a horſe Ile be, ſometime a hound,   (bryer:
A hogge, a headeleſſe Beare, ſometime a fier,
And neigh, and barke, and grunt, and rore, and burne,
Like horſe, hound, hogge, beare, fire, at euery turne. *Exit.*

Bott. Why doe they runne away? This is a knauery of
them to make mee afeard.   *Enter* Snowte.

Sn. O Bottom, thou art chaung'd. What do I ſee on thee?

Bot. What doe you ſee? You ſee an Aſſe head of your
owne. Do you?

Enter Quince.   (*Exit.*

Quin. Bleſſe thee *Bottom*, bleſſe thee. Thou art trãſlated.

Bot. I ſee their knauery. This is to make an aſſe of mee, to
fright me, if they could: but I wil not ſtirre from this place,
do what they can. I will walke vp and downe heere, and I
will ſing, that they ſhall heare I am not afraide.
The Wooſell cock, ſo blacke of hewe,
With Orange tawny bill,

The

The Throstle, with his note so true,
The Wren, with little quill.

 Tytania. What Angell wakes me from my flowry bed?

 Bot. The Fynch, the Sparrowe, and the Larke,
The plainsong Cuckow gray:
Whose note, full many a man doth marke,
And dares not answere, nay.
For indeede, who would set his wit to so foolish a birde?
Who would giue a bird the ly, though hee cry Cuckow,
neuer so?

 Tita. I pray thee, gentle mortall, sing againe.
Myne eare is much enamoured of thy note:
So is mine eye enthralled to thy shape,
And thy faire vertues force (perforce) doth mooue mee,
On the first viewe to say, to sweare, I loue thee.

 Bott. Mee thinks mistresse, you should haue little reason
for that. And yet, to say the truth, reason and loue keepe
little company together, now a daies. The more the pitty,
that some honest neighbours will not make them friends.
Nay I can gleeke, vpon occasion.

 Tyta. Thou art as wise, as thou art beautifull.

 Bott. Not so neither: but if I had wit enough to get out
of this wood, I haue enough to serue mine owe turne.

 Tyta. Out of this wood, doe not desire to goe:
Thou shalt remaine here, whether thou wilt or no.
I am a spirit, of no common rate:
The Sommer, still, doth tend vpon my state,
And I doe loue thee: therefore goe with mee.
Ile giue thee Fairies to attend on thee:
And they shall setch thee Iewels, from the deepe,
And sing, while thou, on pressed flowers, dost sleepe:
And I will purge thy mortall grossenesse so,
That thou shalt, like an ayery spirit, goe.
Pease-blossome, Cobweb, Moth, and *Mustard-seede?*

   Enter foure Fairyes.
  D 3   *Fai-*

Fairies. Readie: and I, and I, and I. Where shall we goe?

Tita. Be kinde and curteous to this gentleman,
Hop in his walkes, and gambole in his eyes,
Feede him with Apricocks, and Dewberries,
With purple Grapes, greene figges, and Mulberries,
The hony bagges steale from the humble Bees,
And for night tapers, croppe their waxen thighes,
And light them at the fiery Glowe-wormes eyes,
To haue my loue to bedde, and to arise,
And pluck the wings, from painted Butterflies,
To fanne the Moone-beames from his sleeping eyes,
Nod to him Elues, and doe him curtesies.

1. *Fai.* Haile mortall, haile.

2. *Fai.* Haile.

3. *Fai.* Haile.

Bot. I cry your worships mercy, hartily : I beseech your
worshippes name.

Cob. Cobwebbe.

Bot. I shall desire you of more acquaintance, good master *Cobweb*: if I cut my finger, I shall make bolde with
you. Your name honest gentleman?

Pea. Pease-blossome.

Bot. I pray you commend mee to mistresse *Squash*, your
mother, and to master *Peascod*, your father. Good master
Pease-blossome, I shall desire you of more acquaintance,
to. Your name I beseech you sir?

Must. Mustardseede.

Bot. Good master *Mustardseede*, I know your patience
well. That same cowardly, gyantlike, Ox-beefe hath de-
uourd many a gentleman of your house. I promise you,
your kindred hath made my eyes water, ere now. I desire
you more acquaintance, good master *Mustardseede*.

Tita. Come waite vpon him : leade him to my bower.
The Moone, me thinkes, lookes with a watry eye:
And when shee weepes, weepes euery little flower,

Lamen-

Lamenting some enforced chastitie.

Ty vp my louers tongue, bring him silently.   *Exit.*   1020

    Enter King of Fairies, *and* Robin goodfellow.   1021

  Ob. I wonder if *Titania* be awak't;

Then what it was, that next came in her eye,

Which she must dote on, in extreamitie.   1024

Here comes my messenger. How now, mad spirit?   1026

What nightrule now about this haunted groue?

  Puck. My mistresse with a monster is in loue,

Neere to her close and consecrated bower.

While she was in her dull, and sleeping hower,   1030

A crew of patches, rude Mechanicals,

That worke for bread, vpon *Athenian* stalles,

Were met together to rehearse a play,

Intended for great *Theseus* nuptiall day: 1000

The shallowest thickskinne, of that barraine sort,

Who *Pyramus* presented, in their sport,

Forsooke his Scene, and entred in a brake,

VVhen I did him at this aduantage take:

An Asses nole I fixed on his head.

Anon his *Thisbie* must be answered,   1040

And forth my Minnick comes. When they him spy,

As wilde geese, that the creeping Fouler eye,

Or russet pated choughes, many in sort

(Rysing, and cawing, at the gunnes report)

Seuer themselues, and madly sweepe the sky:

So, at his sight, away his fellowes fly,

And at our stampe, here ore and ore, one falles:

He murther cryes, and helpe from *Athens* cals.

Their sense, thus weake, lost with their feares, thus strong,

Made senselesse things begin to doe them wrong.   1050

For, briers and thornes, at their apparell, snatch:

Some sleeues, some hats; from yeelders, all things catch.

I led them on, in this distracted feare,

And left sweete *Pyramus* translated there:

When in that moment (so it came to passe)
Tytania wak't, and straight way lou'd an Asse.

  Ob. This falles out better, then I could deuise.
But hast thou yet latcht the *Athenians* eyes,
With the loue iuice, as I did bid thee doe?

  Rob. I tooke him sleeping (that is finisht to)
And the *Athenian* woman, by his side;
That when he wak't, of force she must be ey'd.

        Enter Demetrius *and* Hermia.

  Ob. Stand close: this is the same *Athenian.*

  Rob. This is the woman: but not this the man.

  Demet. O, Why rebuke you him, that loues you so?
Lay breath so bitter, on your bitter foe.

  Her. Now I but chide : but I should vse thee worse,
For thou (I feare) hast giuen me cause to curse.
If thou hast slaine *Lysander*, in his sleepe;   (to.
Being ore shooes in blood, plunge in the deepe, & kill mee
The Sunne was not so true vnto the day,
As hee to mee. Would hee haue stollen away,
Frow sleeping *Hermia?* Ile beleeue, as soone,
This whole earth may be bor'd, and that the Moone
May through the Center creepe, and so displease
Her brothers noonetide, with th' *Antipodes.*
It cannot be, but thou hast murdred him.
So should a murtherer looke; so dead, so grimme.

  Dem. So should the murthered looke, and so should *I,*
Pearst through the heart, with your sterne cruelty.
Yet you, the murtherer, looke as bright, as cleere,
As yonder *Venus*, in her glimmering spheare.

  Her. Whats this to my *Lysander?* Where is hee?
Ah good *Demetrius*, wilt thou giue him mee?

  Deme. I had rather giue his carcasse to my hounds.

  Her. Out dog, out curre : thou driu'st me past the bounds
Of maidens patience. Hast thou slaine him then?
Henceforth be neuer numbred among men.

                        O,

O, once tell true:tell true, euen for my ſake:
Durſt thou haue lookt vpon him, being awake?
And haſt thou kild him, ſleeping? O braue tutch!
Could not a worme, an Adder do ſo much?
An Adder did it: For with doubler tongue
Then thyne (thou ſerpent) neuer Adder ſtung.

 Deme. You ſpende your paſſion, on a miſpriſ'd mood:
I am not guilty of *Lyſanders* bloode:
Nor is he deade, for ought that I can tell.

 Her. I pray thee, tell mee then, that he is well.

 De. And if I could, what ſhould I get therefore?

 Her. A priuiledge, neuer to ſee mee more:
And from thy hated preſence part I: ſee me no more;
Whether he be dead or no.   *Exit.*

 Deme. There is no following her in this fierce vaine.
Heere therefore, for a while, I will remaine.
So ſorrowes heauineſſe doth heauier growe.
For debt that bankrout ſlippe doth ſorrow owe:
Which now in ſome ſlight meaſure it will pay;
If for his tender here I make ſome ſtay.   *Ly doune.*

 Ob. What haſt thou done? Thou haſt miſtaken quite,
And laid the loue iuice on ſome true loues ſight.
Of thy miſpriſion, muſt perforce enſue
Some true loue turnd, and not a falſe turnd true.

 Robi. Then fate orerules, that one man holding troth,
A million faile, confounding oath on oath.

 Ob. About the wood, goe ſwifter then the winde,
And *Helena* of *Athens* looke thou finde.
All fancy ſicke ſhe is and pale of cheere,
With ſighes of loue, that coſts the freſh blood deare.
By ſome illuſion ſee thou bring her here:
Ile charme his eyes, againſt ſhe doe appeare.

 Robin. I goe, I goe, looke how I goe.
Swifter then arrow, from the *Tartars* bowe.

 Ob. Flower of this purple dy,
     E   Exit

1060

1070

1080

1090

1100

1110

1120

1124

Hit with *Cupids* archery,
Sinke in apple of his eye,
When his loue he doth espy,
Let her shine as glorioufly
As the *Venus* of the sky.
When thou wak'ft, if she be by,
Begge of her, for remedy.

                Enter Puck.

Puck. Captaine of our Fairy band,
Helena is heere at hande,
And the youth, miftooke by mee,
Pleading for a louers fee.
Shall wee their fond pageant fee?
Lord, what fooles thefe mortals bee!

  Ob. Stand afide. The noyfe, they make,
Will caufe *Demetrius* to awake,

  Pu. Then will two, at once, wooe one:
That muft needes be fport alone.
And thofe things do beft pleafe mee,
That befall prepoft'roufly.

          Enter Lyfander, *and* Helena.

  Lyf. Why should you think, that I should wooe in fcorne?
Scorne, and derifion, neuer come in teares.
Looke when I vow, I weepe : and vowes fo borne,
In their natiuitie all truth appeares,
How can thefe things, in mee, feeme fcorne to you?
Bearing the badge of faith to prooue them true,

  Hel. You doe aduance your cunning, more, and more,
When trueth killes truth, ô diuelifh holy fray!
Thefe vowes are *Hermias.* Will you giue her ore?
Weigh oath, with oath, and you will nothing waigh.
Your vowes to her, and mee (put in two fcales)
Will euen weigh; and both as light as tales.

  Lyf. I had no iudgement, when to her I fwore:
  Hel. Nor none, in my minde, now you giue her ore.

                                  Lyf.

1130
1140
1150
1160
1100
1110
1120

Lyf. *Demetrius* loues her: and he loues not you.

Deme. O *Helen,* goddeſſe, nymph, perfect diuine,
To what, my loue, ſhall I compare thine eyne!
Chriſtall is muddy. O, how ripe, in ſhowe,
Thy lippes, thoſe kiſſing cherries, tempting growe!
That pure coniealed white, high *Taurus* ſnow,
Fand with the Eaſterne winde, turnes to a crowe,
When thou holdſt vp thy hand, O, let me kiſſe
This Princeſſe of pure white, this ſeale of bliſſe.

Hel. O ſpight! O hell! I ſee, you all are bent
To ſet againſt mee, for your merriment.
If you were ciuill, and knew curteſie,
You would not doe mee thus much iniury.
Can you not hate mee, as I know you doe,
But you muſt ioyne, in ſoules, to mocke mee to?
If you were men, as men you are in ſhowe,
You would not vſe a gentle Lady ſo;
To vowe, and ſweare, and ſuperpraiſe my parts,
When I am ſure, you hate mee with your hearts.
You both are Riuals, and loue *Hermia:*
And now both Riualles, to mock *Helena.*
A trim exploit, a manly enterpriſe,
To coniure teares vp, in a poore maides eyes,
With your deriſion None, of noble ſort,
Would ſo offend a virgine, and extort
A poore ſoules patience, all to make you ſport.

Lyſand, You are vnkinde, *Demetrius:* be not ſo.
For you loue *Hermia:* this you know I know.
And heare, with all good will, with all my heart,
In *Hermias* loue I yeelde you vp my part:
And yours of *Helena,* to mee bequeath:
Whom I doe loue, and will do till my death.

Hel. Neuer did mockers waſte more idle breath.

Deme. *Lyſander,* keepe thy *Hermia:* I will none.
If ere I lou'd her, all that loue is gone.

E 2   My

My heart to her, but as gueſtwiſe, ſoiournd:
And now to *Helen*, is it home returnd,
There to remaine.

 Lyſ. Helen, it is not ſo.

 Deme. Diſparage not the faith, thou doſt not know;
Leaſt to thy perill, thou aby it deare.
Looke where thy loue comes : yonder is thy deare.

    Enter Hermia.

 Her. Darke night, that from the eye, his function takes,
The eare more quicke of apprehenſion makes.
Wherein it doth impaire the ſeeing ſenſe,
It payes the hearing double recompence.
Thou art not, by myne eye, *Lyſander*, found:
Mine eare, I thanke it, brought me to thy ſound.
But why, vnkindly, didſt thou leaue mee ſo?

 Lyſ. Why ſhould he ſtay, whom loue doth preſſe to go?

 Her. What loue could preſſe *Lyſander*, from my ſide?

 Lyſ. Lyſanders loue(that would not let him bide)
Faire *Helena* : who more engilds the night
Then all yon fiery oes, and eyes of light.
Why ſeek'ſt thou me? Could not this make thee know,
The hate I bare thee, made mee leaue thee ſo?

 Her. You ſpeake not as you thinke : It cannot bee.

 Hel. Lo : ſhe is one of this confederacy.
Now I perceiue, they haue conioynd all three,
To faſhion this falſe ſport, in ſpight of mee.
Iniurious *Hermia*, moſt vngratefull maide,
Haue you conſpir'd, haue you with theſe contriu'd
To baite mee, with this foule deriſion?
Is all the counſell that we two haue ſhar'd,
The ſiſters vowes, the howers that we haue ſpent,
When we haue chid the haſtie footed time,
For parting vs; O, is all forgot?
All ſchooldaies friendſhippe, childhood innocence?
VVee, *Hermia*, like two artificiall gods,

         Haue

Haue with our needles, created both one flower,
Both on one ſampler, ſitting on one cuſhion,
Both warbling of one ſong, both in one key;
As if our hands, our ſides, voyces, and mindes
Had bin incorporate. So wee grewe together,
Like to a double cherry, ſeeming parted;
But yet an vnion in partition,
Two louely berries moulded on one ſtemme:
So with two ſeeming bodies, but one heart,
Two of the firſt life coats in heraldry,
Due but to one, and crowned with one creaſt.
And will you rent our auncient loue aſunder,
To ioyne with men, in ſcorning your poore friend?
It is not friendly, tis not maidenly.
Our ſex, as well as I, may chide you for it;
Though I alone doe ſele the iniury.
 Her. I am amazed at your words:
I ſcorne you not. It ſeemes that you ſcorne mee,
 Hel. Haue you not ſet *Lyſander*, as in ſcorne,
To follow mee, and praiſe my eyes and face?
And made your other loue, *Demetrius*
(Who euen but now did ſpurne mee with his foote)
To call mee goddeſſe, nymph, diuine, and rare,
Pretious celeſtiall? VVherefore ſpeakes he this,
To her he hates? And wherfore doth *Lyſander*
Deny your loue (ſo rich within his ſoule)
And tender mee (forſooth) affection,
But by your ſetting on, by your conſent?
VVhat, though I be not ſo in grace as you,
So hung vpon with loue, ſo fortunate?
(But miſerable moſt, to loue vnlou'd)
This you ſhould pittie, rather then deſpiſe.
 Her. I vnderſtand not, what you meane by this.
 Hel. I doe. Perſeuer, counterfait ſad lookes:
Make mouthes vpon mee, when I turne my back: VVinke
   E 2

37

Winke each at other, holde the ſweeete ieaſt vp.
This ſport well carried, ſhall bee chronicled.
If you haue any pitty, grace, or manners,
You would not make mee ſuch an argument.
But fare ye well : tis partly my owne fault :
Which death, or abſence ſoone ſhall remedy.

Lyſ. Stay, gentle *Helena* : heare my excuſe,
My loue, my life, my ſoule, faire *Helena*.

Hel. O excellent!

Herm. Sweete, doe not ſcorne her ſo.

Dem. If ſhe cannot entreat, I can compell.

Lyſ. Thou canſt compell no more, then ſhe intreat.
Thy threats haue no more ſtrength then her weake praiſe.
Helen, I loue thee, by my life I doe :
I ſweare by that which I will looſe for thee ;
To prooue him falſe, that ſaies I loue thee not.

Dem. I ſay, I loue thee more then he can do.

Lyſ. If thou ſay ſo, withdrawe, and prooue it to.

Dem. Quick come.

Her. *Lyſander,* whereto tends all this?

Lyſ. Away, you *Ethiop*.

Dem. No, no : heele
Seeme to breake looſe : take on as you would follow ;
But yet come not. You are a tame man, go.

Lyſ. Hang of thou cat, thou bur : vile thing let looſe ;
Or I will ſhake thee from mee, like a ſerpent.

Her. Why are you growne ſo rude? What change is this,
Sweete loue?

Lyſ. Thy loue? Out tawny *Tartar,* out :
Out loathed medcine : ô hated potion hence.

Her. Doe you not ieaſt?

Hel. Yes ſooth : and ſo doe you.

Lyſ. *Demetrius,* I will keepe my word, with thee.

Dem. I would I had your bond. For I perceiue,
A weake bond holds you. Ile not truſt your word.

Lyſ.

1270

1280

1290

1300

1240

1250

1260

38

Lyſ. What? ſhould I hurt her, ſtrike her, kill her dead?
Although I hate her, Ile not harme her ſo.

Her. What? Can you do me greater harme, then hate?
Hate mee, wherefore? O me, what newes, my loue?
Am not I *Hermia*? Are not you *Lyſander*?
I am as faire now, as I was ere while.
Since night, you lou'd mee; yet ſince night, you left mee,
Why then, you left mee (ô the gods forbid)
In earneſt, ſhall I ſay?

Lyſ. I , by my life:
And neuer did deſire to ſee thee more.
Theſore be out of hope, of queſtion, of doubt:
Be certaine : nothing truer : tis no ieaſt,
That I doe hate thee, and loue *Helena*.

Her. O mee, you iuggler, you canker bloſſome,
You theeſe of loue : what, haue you come by night,
And ſtolne my loues heart, from him?

Hel. Fine, I faith.
Haue you no modeſty, no maiden ſhame,
No touch of baſhfulneſſe? Whar, will you teare
Impatient anſweres, from my gentle tongue?
Fy, ſy, you counterfait, you puppet, you.

Her. Puppet? Why ſo? I , that way goes the game.
Now I perceiue that ſhe hath made compare,
Betweene our ſtatures, ſhe hath vrg'd her height,
And with her perſonage, her tall perſonage,
Her height (forſooth) ſhe hath preuaild with him.
And are you growne ſo high in his eſteeme,
Becauſe I am ſo dwarfiſh and ſo lowe?
How lowe am I , thou painted May-pole? Speake:
How lowe am I ? I am not yet ſo lowe,
But that my nailes can reach vnto thine eyes.

Hel. I pray you, though you mocke me, gentleman,
Let her not hurt me, I was neuer curſt:
I haue no gift at all in ſhrewiſhneſſe:

E 4

I am a right maid, for my cowardize:
Let her not ftrike mee. You perhaps, may thinke,
Becaufe fhe is fomething lower then my felfe,
That I can match her.

    *Her.*Lower? harke againe.

    Hel. Good *Hermia,* do not be fo bitter with mee,
I euermore did loue you *Hermia,*
Did euer keepe your counfels, neuer wrongd you;
Saue that in loue, vnto *Demetrius,*
I tould him of your ftealth vnto this wood.
He followed you : for loue, I followed him.
But he hath chid me hence, and threatned mee
To ftrike mee, fpurne mee; nay to kill mee to.
And now, fo you will let me quiet goe,
To *Athens* will I beare my folly backe,
And follow you no further. Let me goe.
You fee how fimple, and how fond I am.

    Herm. Why? get you gon. Who ift that hinders you?

    Hel. A foolifh heart, that I leaue here behind.

    Her. What, with *Lyfander?*

    Hel. With *Demetrius.*

    Lyf. Be not afraid: fhe fhall not harme thee *Helena.*

    Deme. No fir: fhe fhall not, though you take her part.

    Hel. O, when fhe is angry, fhe is keene and fhrewd.
She was a vixen, when fhe went to fchoole :
And though fhe be but little, fhe is fierce.

    Her. Little againe? Nothing hut low and little?
Why will you fuffer her to floute me thus?
Let me come to her.

    Lyf. Get you gon, you dwarfe;
You *minimus,* of hindring knot graffe, made;
You bead, you acorne.

    Deme. You are too officious,
In her behalfe, that fcornes your feruices.
Let her alone: fpeake not of *Helena,*

                                          Take

Take not her part . For if thou doſt intend
Neuer ſo little ſhewe of loue to her,
Thou ſhalt aby it.

    Lyſ. Now ſhe holdes me not:
Now follow, if thou dar'ſt, to try whoſe right,
Of thine or mine, is moſt in *Helena.*

    Deme. Follow? Nay: Ile go with thee, cheeke by iowle.

    Her. You, miſtreſſe, all this coyle is long of you.
Nay: goe not backe.

    Hel. I will not truſt you, I,
Nor longer ſtay in your curſt company.
Your hands, than mine, are quicker for a fray:
My legges are longer though, to runne away.

    Her. I am amaz'd, and know not what to ſay. *Exeunt.*

    Ob. This is thy negligence: ſtill thou miſtak'ſt,
Or elſe commitſt thy knaueries wilfully.

    Puck. Beleeue mee, king of ſhadowes, I miſtooke.
Did not you tell mee, I ſhoud know the man,
By the *Athenian* garments, he had on?
And, ſo farr e blameleſſe prooue's my enterpriſe,
That I haue nointed an *Athenians* eyes:
And ſo farre am I glad, it ſo did ſort,
As this their iangling I eſteeme a ſport.

    Ob. Thou ſeeſt, theſe louers ſeeke a place to fight:
Hy therefore *Robin,* ouercaſt the night,
The ſtarry welkin couer thou anon,
With drooping fogge as blacke as *Acheron,*
And lead theſe teaſty Riuals ſo aſtray,
As one come not within anothers way.
Like to *Lyſander,* ſometime frame thy tongue:
Then ſtirre *Demetrius* vp, with bitter wrong:
And ſometime raile thou like *Demetriue:*
And from each other, looke thou lead them thus;
Till ore their browes, death-counterfaiting, ſleepe,
With leaden legs, and Batty wings doth creepe:

    F   Then

1340
1350
1360
1370
1377–8
1380
1384
1384+
1386
1390
1400

Then crush this hearbe into *Lysanders* eye;
Whose liquor hath this vertuous property,
To take from thence all errour, with his might,
And make his eyebals roule with wonted sight,
When they next wake, all this derision
Shall seeme a dreame, and fruitelesse vision,
And backe to *Athens* shall the louers wend,
With league, whose date, till death shall neuer end,
Whiles I, in this affaire, doe thee imploy,
Ile to my Queene and beg her *Indian* boy:
And then I will her charmed eye release
From monsters viewe, and all things shall be peace.
  Puck. My Faiery Lord, this must be done with haste.
For nights swift Dragons cut the clouds full fast,
And yonder shines *Auroras* harbinger:
At whose approach, Ghosts, wandring here and there,
Troope home to Churchyards: damned spirits all,
That in crosse waies and floods haue buriall,
Already to their wormy beds are gone:
For feare least day should looke their shames vpon,
They wilfully themselues exile from light,
And must for aye consort with black browed night.
  Ober. But we are spirits of another sort.
I, with the mornings loue, haue oft made sport,
And like a forrester, the groues may tread
Euen till the Easterne gate all fiery red,
Opening on *Neptune*, with faire blessed beames,
Turnes, into yellow golde, his salt greene streames,
But notwistanding, haste, make no delay:
We may effect this businesse, yet ere day.
  Pu. Vp & down, vp & down, I will lead them vp & down:
I am feard in field & town. *Goblin*, lead them vp & downe.
Here comes one.   *Enter* Lysander.
  Lys. Where art thou, proud *Demetrius?* Speak thou now,
  Rob. Here villaine, drawne & ready. Where art thou?
                                                    Lys.

Lyf. I will be with thee ſtraight.

Rob. Follow me then to plainer ground.

Enter Demetrius.

Deme. Lyſander, ſpeake againe,
Thou runaway, thou coward, art thou fled?
Speake in ſome buſh, Where doeſt thou hide thy head?

Rob. Thou coward art thou bragging, to the ſtarres,
Telling the buſhes that thou look'ſt for warres,
And wilt not come? Come recreant, come thou childe,
Ile whippe thee with a rodde. He is defil'd,
That drawes a ſword on thee.

De. Yea, art thou there?

Ro. Follow my voice: weele try no manhood here. *Exeut.*

Lyf. He goes before me, and ſtill dares me on:
When I come where he calles, then he is gon.
The villaine is much lighter heel'd then I;
I followed faſt: but faſter he did fly;
That fallen am I in darke vneauen way,
And here will reſt me. Come thou gentle day,
For if but once, thou ſhewe me thy gray light,
Ile finde *Demetrius,* and reuenge this ſpight.

Robin, *and* Demetrius.

Robi. HO, ho, ho: Coward, why comſt thou not?

Deme. Abide me, if thou darſt, For well I wot,
Thou runſt before mee, ſhifting euery place,
And dar'ſt not ſtand, nor looke me in the face,
Where art thou now?

Rob. Come hither: I am here.

De. Nay then thou mockſt me, Thou ſhat buy this dear,
if euer I thy face by day light ſee.
Now, goe thy way. Faintneſſe conſtraineth mee,
To meaſure, out my length, on this cold bed:
By daies approach looke to be viſited.

Enter Helena.

Hele. O weary night, O long and tedious night,

F 2   Abate

1480 Abate thy houres, shine comforts, from the east;
That I may backe to *Athens*, by day light,
From these that my poore company detest:
And sleepe, that sometimes shuts vp sorrowes eye,
Steale mee a while from mine owne companie. *Sleepe.*
  Rob Yet but three? Come one more.
Two of both kindes makes vp sower.
Heare shee comes, curst and sadde.
1488 *Cupid* is a knauish ladde,
1490 Thus to make poore females madde.   1450
  Her. Neuer so weary, neuer so in woe,
Bedabbled with the deaw, and torne with briers:
I can no further crawle, no further goe:
My legges can keepe no paie with my desires,
Here will I rest mee, till the breake of day:
Heauens shielde *Lysander*, if they meane a fray.
  Rob. On the ground, sleepe sound:
Ile apply your eye, gentle louer, remedy.
When thou wak't, thou tak'st
1500 True delight, in the sight, of thy former ladies eye: 1460
And the country prouerbe knowne,
That euery man should take his owne,
In your waking shall be showen.
Iacke shall haue *Iill*: nought shall goe ill:
1505-6 The man shall haue his mare again, & all shall be well.
1509   *Enter Queene of* Faeries, *and Clowne, and* Faieries: and
1510   *the king behinde them.*
  Tita. Come sit thee downe vpon this flowry bed,
While I thy amiable cheekes doe coy,
And stick musk roses in thy sleeke smooth head,   1470
And kisse thy faire large eares, my gentle ioy.
  Clown. Where's *Pease-blossome*?
  Pea. Ready.
  Clow. Scratch my heade, *Pease-blossome*. Wher's Moun-
1518-19 sieur *Cobweb*? *Cob.* Ready.

                                                Clo.

44

Clo. Mounsieur *Cobweb*, good Mounsieur, get you your
weapons in your hand, and kill me a red hipt Humble Bee,
on the toppe of a thistle : and good Mounsieur, bring mee
the hony bagge. Doe not fret your selfe too much, in the
action, Mounsieur : and good Mounsieur haue a care, the
honybagge breake not, I wold be loath to haue you ouer-
flowen with a honibag *signior*. Where's Mounsieur *Mustardseede?*

Must. Readie.

Clo. Giue me your neafe, Mounsieur *Mustardseede*, Pray
you, leaue your curtsie, good Mounsieur.

Must. what's your will?

Clo. Nothing good Mounsieur, but to helpe Caualery
Cobwebbe, to scratch, I must to the Barbers , Mounsieur,
For me thinkes I am maruailes hairy about the face. And I
am such a tender Asse, if my haire doe but tickle mee, I
must scratch.

Tita. What, wilt thou heare some musique, my sweete
loue?

Clo. I haue a reasonable good eare in musique, Lets
haue the tongs, and the bones.

Tyta. Or, say sweete loue, what thou desirest to eate.

Clo. Truely a pecke of prouander. I could mounch your
good dry Oates. Me thinkes, I haue a great desire to a bot-
tle of hay. Good hay, sweete hay hath no fellow. (hoord,

Ty. I haue a venturous Fairy, that shall seeke the Squirils
And fetch thee newe nuts.

Clo. I had rather haue a handfull, or two of dryed pease.
But, I pray you let none of your people stirre me: I haue an
exposition of sleepe come vpon mee.

Tyta. Sleepe thou, and I will winde thee in my armes,
Faieries be gon, and be alwaies away.
So doth the woodbine, the sweete Honisuckle,
Gently entwist: the female Iuy so
Enrings the barky fingers of the Elme,

F 3

A Midsommer nightes dreame.

O how I loue thee! how I dote on thee!

Enter Robin goodfellow.

Ob. Welcome good *Robin.* Seeſt thou this ſweete ſight?
Her dotage now I doe beginne to pittie.
For meeting her of late, behinde the wood,
Seeking ſweete fauours for this hatefull foole,
I did vpbraid her, and fall out with her.
For ſhe his hairy temples then had rounded,
With coronet of freſh and fragrant flowers.
And that ſame deawe which ſometime on the buddes,
Was wont to ſwell, like round and orient pearles;
Stood now within the pretty flouriets eyes,
Like teares, that did their owne diſgrace bewaile.
When I had, at my pleaſure, taunted her,
And ſhe, in milde te armes, begd my patience,
I then did aske of her, her changeling childe:
Which ſtraight ſhe gaue mee, and her Fairy ſent
To beare him, to my bower, in Fairie land.
And now I haue the boy, I will vndoe
This hatefull imperfection of her eyes.
And, gentle *Puck*, take this transformed ſcalpe,
From of the heade of this *Athenian* ſwaine;
That hee, awaking when the other do,
May all to *Athens* backe againe repaire,
And thinke no more of this nights accidents,
But as the fearce vexation of a dreame.
But firſt I will releaſe the Fairy Queene.
    Be, as thou waſt wont to bee:
    See, as thou waſt wont to ſee.
    Dians budde, or *Cupids* flower,
    Hath ſuch force, and bleſſed power.
Now, my *Titania*, wake you, my ſweete Queene.
Tita. My *Oberon*, what viſions haue I ſeene!
Me thought I was enamourd of an Aſſe.
    Ob. There lyes your loue.

                                    Tita.

1559
1560-1

1520

1570

1530

1580

1540

1590

Tita. How came these things to passe?
O, how mine eyes doe loath his visage now!
  Ob. Silence a while. *Robin*, take off this head:
Titania , musicke call, and strike more dead
Then common sleepe: of all these, fine the sense.
Ti. Musick, howe musick: such as charmeth sleepe. (peepe.
  Rob. Now, when thou wak'st, with thine own fools eyes
Ob. Sound Musick: come, my queen, take hands with me,
And rocke the ground whereon these sleepers be.
Now, thou and I are new in amitie,
And will to morrow midnight, solemnely
Daunce, in Duke *Theseus* house triumphantly,
And blesse it to all faire prosperitie.
There shall the paires of faithfull louers be
Wedded, with *Theseus*, all in iollitie.
  Rob. Fairy King, attend, and marke:
I do heare the morning Larke.
  Ob. Then my Queene, in silence sad,
Trippe we after nights shade:
We, the Globe, can compasse soone,
Swifter then the wandring Moone.
  Tita. Come my Lord, and in our flight,
Tell me how it came this night,
That I sleeping here was found,
With these mortals on the ground.   *Exeunt.*
  Enter Theseus *and all his traine.*   *VVinde horne.*
  The. Goe one of you, finde out the forrester:
For now our obseruation is performde.
And since we haue the vaward of the day,
My loue shall heare the musicke of my hounds.
Vncouple, in the westerne vallie, let them goe:
Dispatch I say, and finde the forrester,
Wee will, faire Queene, vp to the mountaines toppe,
And marke the musicall confusion
Of hounds and Echo in coniunction.
                    F 4   *Hippoli.*

1550
1560
1570
1580

1599
1601–2

1610

1619
1621
1622–3

1630

Hip. I was with Hercules and *Cadmus*, once,
When in a wood of *Creete* they bayed the Beare,
With hounds of *Sparta* : neuer did I heare
Such gallant chiding. For besides the groues,
The skyes, the fountaines, euery region neare
Seeme all one mutuall cry. I neuer heard
So musicall a discord, such sweete thunder.

Thes. My hounds are bred out of the *Spartane* kinde:
So flew'd, so sanded: and their heads are hung
VVith eares, that sweepe away the morning deawe,
Crooke kneed, and deawlapt, like *Thessa'ian* Buls:
Slowe in pursuit; but matcht in mouth like bels,
Each vnder each. A cry more tunable
Was neuer hollowd to, nor cheerd with horne,
In *Creete*, in *Sparta*, nor in *Thessaly*.
Iudge when you heare. But soft. What nymphes are these?

Egeus. My Lord, this my daughter heere a sleepe,
And this *Lysander*, this *Demetrius* is,
This *Helena*, old *Nedars Helena*.
I wonder of their being here together.

The. No doubt, they rose vp earely, to obserue
The right of May : and hearing our intent,
Came heere, in grace of our solemnitie.
But speake, *Egeus*, is not this the day,
That *Hermia* should giue answer of her choyce?

Egeus. It is, my Lord.   (hornes.
These. Goe, bid the huntsmen wake them with their
            Shoute within: they all start vp. Winde hornes.

The. Good morrow, friends. Saint *Valentine* is past.
Begin these wood birds but to couple, now?

Lys. Pardon, my Lord.

The. I pray you all, stand vp.
I know, you two are Riuall enemies.
How comes this gentle concord in the worlde,
That hatred is so farre from iealousie,

                                                    To

To sleepe by hate, and feare no enmitie,   1670
  Lyſ. My Lord, I ſhal reply amazedly,
Halfe ſleepe, halfe waking, But, as yet, I ſweare,
I cannot truely ſay how I came here,
But as I thinke (for truely would I ſpeake)
And now I doe bethinke mee, ſo it is;
I came with *Hermia*, hither, Our intent
Was to be gon from *Athens*: where we might
Without the perill of the *Athenian* lawe,
  Ege. Enough, enough my Lord : you haue enough.   1680
I begge the law, the law, vpon his head:
They would haue ſtolne away, they would, *Demetrius,*
Thereby to haue defeated you and me:
You of your wife, and mee, of my conſent:
Of my conſent, that ſhe ſhould be your wife.
  Deme. My Lord, faire *Helen* told me of their ſtealth,
Of this their purpoſe hither, to this wood,
And I in fury hither followed them;
Faire Helena, in fancy following mee.
But my good Lord, I wote not by what power   1690
(But by ſome power it is)my loue,
To *Hermia* (melted as the ſnowe)
Seemes to me now as the remembrance of an idle gaude,
Which in my childehoode I did dote vpon:
And all the faith, the vertue of my heart,
The obiect and the pleaſure of mine eye,
Is onely Helena. To her, my Lord,
Was I betrothed, ere I ſee *Hermia*:
But, like a ſickneſſe, did I loath this foode,
But, as in health, come to my naturall taſte,   1700
Now I doe wiſh it, loue it, long for it,
And will for euermore be true to it.
  The. Faire louers, you are fortunately met,
Of this diſcourſe, we more will here anon,

                        G   *Egeus,*

Egeus, I will ouerbeare your will: 1650
For in the Temple, by and by, with vs,
Theſe couples ſhall eternally be knit.
And, for the morning now is ſomthing worne,
Our purpoſ'd hunting ſhall be ſet aſide.
Away, with vs, to *Athens*. Three and three,
Weele holde a feaſt, in great ſolemnitie, Come *Hyppolita*. 1710–11
  Deme. Theſe things ſeeme ſmall and vndiſtinguiſhable,
Like farre off mountaines turned into clouds.
  Her. Me thinks I ſee theſe things, with parted eye,
When euery thing ſeemes double. 1660
  Hel. So mee thinkes:
And I haue fonnd *Demetrius*, like a iewell,
Mine owne, and not mine owne.
  Dem. Are you ſure +1
That we are awake? It ſeemes to me, +1
That yet we ſleepe, we dreame. Do not you thinke, 1720
The Duke was here, and bid vs follow him?
  Her. Yea, and my father.
  Hel. And *Hyppolita*.
  Lyſ. And he did bid vs follow to the Temple. 1670
  Dem. Why then, we are awake: lets follow him, and by
the way lets recount our dreames. 1726
  Clo. When my cue comes, call mee, and I will anſwere. 1728
My next is, moſt faire *Pyramus*. Hey ho. *Peeter Quince*?
Flute, the bellowes mender? *Snout* the tinker? *Starueling*? 1730
Gods my life! Stolne hence, and left mee a ſleepe? I haue
had a moſt rare viſion. I haue had a dreame, paſt the wit
of man, to ſay; what dreame it was. Man is but an Aſſe, if
hee goe about expound this dreame. Me thought I was,
there is no man can tell what. Me thought I was, and me
thought I had. But man is but patcht a foole, If hee will 1680
offer to ſay, what mee thought I had. The eye of man
hath not heard, the eare of man hath not ſeene, mans
hand

hand is not able to taste, his tongue to conceiue, nor his hearte to report, what my dreame was. I will get Peter Quince to write a Ballet of this dreame: it shall be call'd *Bottoms Dreame*; because it hath no bottome: and I will sing it in the latter end of a Play, before the Duke. Peraduenture, to make it the more gratious, I shall sing it at her death.

Enter Quince, Flute, Thisby *and the rabble.*

Quin. Haue you sent to *Bottoms* house? Is he come home, yet?

Flut. Hee cannot be heard of. Out of doubt he is transported.

Thyf. If hee come not, then the Play is mard. It goes not forward. Doth it?

Quin. It is not possible. You haue not a man, in all *Athens*, able to discharge *Pyramus*, but he.

Thyf. No, hee hath simply the best wit of any handycraft man in *Athens*.

Quin. Yea, and the best person to; and hee is a very Paramour, for a sweete voice.

Thif. You must say, Paragon. A Paramour is (God blesse vs) a thing of nought.

Enter Snug, *the Ioyner.*

Snug. Masters, the Duke is comming from the Temple, and there is two or three Lords and Ladies more married. If our sport had gon forward, wee had all beene made men.

Thyf. O sweete bully *Bottome.* Thus hath hee lost six pence a day, during his life: hee coulde not haue scaped sixe pence a day. And the Duke had not giuen him six pence a day, for playing *Pyramus*, Ile be hanged. He would haue deserued it, Six pence a day, in *Pyramus*, or

G2

51

or nothing.

Enter Bottom.

Bot. Where are these lads? Where are these harts?

Quin, Bottom, ô most couragious day! O most happy houre!

Bott. Masters, I am to discourse wonders: but aske me not what. For if I tell you, I am not true *Athenian.* I will tell you euery thing right as it fell out.

Quin. Let vs heare, sweete *Bottom.*

Bot. Not a word of mee, All that I will tell you, is, that the Duke hath dined. Get your apparrell together, good strings to your beardes, new ribands to your pumpes, meete presently at the palace, euery man looke ore his part. For, the short and the long is, our play is preferd. In any case let *Thisby* haue cleane linnen: and let not him, that plaies the Lyon, pare his nailes: for they shall hang out for the Lyons clawes. And most deare Actors, eate no O-nions, nor garlicke: for we are to vtter sweete breath: and I do not doubt but to hear them say, it is a sweete Comedy. No more wordes. Away, go away.

Enter Theseus, Hyppolita, *and* Philostrate.

Hip. Tis strange, my *Theseus,* that these louers speake of.

The. More straunge then true. I neuer may beleeue These antique fables, nor these Fairy toyes. Louers, and mad men haue such seething braines, Such shaping phantasies, that apprehend more, Then coole reason euer comprehends. The lunatick, The louer, and the Poet are of imagination all compact. One sees more diuels, then vast hell can holde: That is the mad man. The louer, all as frantick, Sees *Helens* beauty in a brow of *Ægypt.* The Poets eye, in a fine frenzy, rolling, doth glance From heauen to earth, from earth to heauen. And as Imagination bodies forth the formes of things

Vn-

52

Vnknowne : the Poets penne turnes them to ſhapes,
And giues to a yery nothing, a locall habitation,
And a name. Such trickes hath ſtrong imagination,
That if it would but apprehend ſome ioy,
It comprehends ſome bringer of that ioy.
Or in the night, imagining ſome feare,
How eaſie is a buſh ſuppoſ'd a Beare?

Hyp. But, all the ſtory of the night told ouer,
And all their minds transfigur'd ſo together,
More witneſſeth than fancies images,
And growes to ſomething of great conſtancy:
But howſoeuer, ſtrange and admirable.

    Enter Louers; Lyſander, Demetrius, Hermia *and*
            Helena.

   The. Here come the louers, full of ioy and mirth.
Ioy, gentle friends, ioy and freſh daies
Of loue accompany your hearts,

   Lyſ. More then to vs, waite in your royall walkes, your
boorde, your bedde.   (haue,

   The. Come now : what maskes, what daunces ſhall wee
To weare away this long age of three hours, betweene
Or after ſupper, & bed-time? Where is our vſuall manager
Of mirth? What Reuels are in hand? Is there no play,
To eaſe the anguiſh of a torturing hower? Call *Philoſtrate.*

   Philoſtrate. Here mighty *Theſeus.*

   The. Say, what abridgement haue you for this euening?
What maske, what muſicke? How ſhall we beguile
The lazy tyme, if not with ſome delight?

   Philoſt. There is a briefe, how many ſports are ripe.
Make choyce, of which your Highneſſe will ſee firſt.

   The. The battell with the *Centaures* to be ſung,
By an *Athenian* Eunuche, to the Harpe?
Weele none of that, That haue I tolde my loue,
In glory of my kinſman *Hercules.*
The ryot of the tipſie *Bachanals,*
               G 3   Tea-

Tearing the *Thracian* ſinger, in their rage?
That is an olde deuiſe : and it was plaid,
When I from *Thebes* came laſt a conquerer.
The thriſe three Muſes, mourning for the death
Oflearning, late deceaſt, in beggery?
That is ſome *Satire* keene and criticall,
Not ſorting with a nuptiall ceremony.
A tedious briefe Scene of young *Pyramus*
And his loue *Thiſby*, very tragicall mirth?
Merry, and tragicall?Tedious, and briefe? That is hot Iſe,
And wōdrous ſtrange ſnow. How ſhall we find the cōcord
Of this diſcord?
  Philoſt. A Play there is, my Lord, ſome ten words long;
Which is as briefe, as I haue knowne a play:
But, by ten words, my Lord it is too long:
Which makes it tedious· For in all the Play,
There is not one word apt, one player fitted.
And tragicall, my noble Lord, it is. For *Pyramus*,
Therein, doth kill himſelfe. Which when I ſaw
Rehearſt, I muſt confeſſe, made mine eyes water:
But more merry teares the paſſion of loud laughter
Neuer ſhed.
  Theſe. What are they, that doe play it?
  Phil. Hard handed men, that worke in *Athens* here,
Which neuer labour'd in their minds till now:
And now haue toyled their vnbreathed memories,
With this ſame Play, againſt your nuptiall.
  The. And wee will heare it.
  Phi. No, my noble Lord, it is not for you. I haue heard
It ouer, and it is nothing, nothing in the world;
Vnleſſe you can finde ſport in their entents,
Extreamely ſtretcht, and cond with cruell paine,
To do you ſeruice.
  The. I will heare that play. For neuer any thing
Can be amiſſe, when ſimpleneſſe and duety tender it.
                                        Goe

Goe bring them in, and take your places, Ladies.

   Hip. I loue not to ſee wretchednesse orecharged;
And duety, in his ſeruice, periſhing.

   The. Why, gentle ſweete, you ſhall ſee no ſuch thing.

   Hip. He ſayes, they can doe nothing in this kinde.

   The. The kinder we, to giue them thanks, for nothing.
Our ſport ſhall be, to take what they miſtake.
And what poore duty cannot doe, noble reſpect
Takes it in might, not merit.
Where I haue come, great Clerkes haue purpoſed
To greete me, with premeditated welcomes;
Where I haue ſeene them ſhiuer and looke pale,
Make periods in the midſt of ſentences,
Throttle their practiz'd accent in their feares,
And in concluſion dumbly haue broke off,
Not paying mee a welcome. Truſt me, ſweete,
Out of this ſilence, yet, I pickt a welcome:
And in the modeſty of fearefull duty,
I read as much, as from the rattling tongue
Of ſaucy and audacious eloquence.
Loue, therefore, and tong-tide ſimplicity,
In leaſt, ſpeake moſt, to my capacity.

   Philoſt. So pleaſe your Grace, the Prologue is addreſt.

   Duk. Let him approach.

Enter the Prologue.

   Pro. If wee offend, it is with our good will.
That you ſhould thinke, we come not to offend,
But with good will.   To ſhew our ſimple skill,
That is the true beginning of our end.
Conſider then, we come but in deſpight.
We doe not come, as minding to content you,
Our true intent is. All for your delight,
Wee are not here. That you ſhould here repent you,
The Actors are at hand: and, by their ſhowe,
You ſhall know all, that you are like to knowe.

G 4

The.

The. This fellow doth not ſtand vpon points.

Lyſ. He hath rid his Prologue, like a rough Colte : hee knowes not the ſtoppe. A good morall my Lord. It is not enough to ſpeake ; but to ſpeake true.

Hyp. Indeed he hath plaid on this Prologue, like a child on a Recorder, a ſound ; but not in gouernement.

The. His ſpeach was like a tangled Chaine ; nothing impaired, but all diſordered. Who is next?

Enter Pyramus, *and* Thisby, *and* Wall, *and* Mooneſhine, *and* Lyon.

Prologue. Gentles, perchance you wonder at this ſhow.
But, wonder on, till truthe make all things plaine,
This man is *Pyramus,* if you would knowe :
This beautious Lady *Thſby* is certaine.
This man, with lyme and roughcaſt, doth preſent
Wall, that vile wall, which did theſe louers ſunder :
And through wals chinke, poore ſoules, they are content
To whiſper. At the which, let no man wonder.
This man, with lanterne, dogge, and buſh of thorne,
Preſenteth moone-ſhine. For if you will know,
By moone-ſhine did theſe louers thinke no ſcorne
To meete at *Ninus* tombe, there, there to wooe:
This grizly beaſt (which Lyon hight by name)
The truſty *Thyſby,* comming firſt by night,
Did ſcarre away, or rather did affright :
And as ſhe fled, her mantle ſhe did fall :
Which Lyon vile with bloody mouth did ſtaine.
Anon comes *Pyramus,* ſweete youth, and tall,
And findes his truſty *Thiſbyes* mantle ſlaine :
Whereat, with blade, with bloody blamefull blade,
He brauely broacht his boyling bloody breaſt,
And *Thiſby,* tarying in Mulberry ſhade,
His dagger drewe, and dyed. For all the reſt,
Let *Lyon, Moone-ſhine, Wall,* and louers twaine,
At large diſcourſe, while here they doe remaine,

The.

The. I wonder, if the Lyon be to speake.

Demet. No wonder, my Lord. One Lyon may, when many Asses doe.

      Exit Lyon, Thysby, *and* Mooneshine.

Wall. In this same enterlude it doth befall,
That I, one *Flute* (by name) present a wall:
And such a wall, as I would haue you thinke
That had in it a cranied hole or chinke:
Through which the louers, *Pyramus*, and *Thisby*,
Did whisper often, very secretly.
This lome, this roughcast, and this stone doth showe,
That I am that same wall : the truth is so.
And this the cranie is, right and sinister,
Through which the fearefull louers are to whisper.

    The. Would you desire lime and haire to speake better?

    Deme. It is the wittiest partition, that euer I heard discourse, my Lord.

    The. *Pyramus* drawes neare the wall: silence.

    Py. O grim lookt night, o night, with hue so blacke,
O night, which euer art, when day is not:
O night, O night, alacke, alacke, alacke,
I feare my *Thisbyes* promise is forgot.
And thou ô wall, ô sweete, ô louely wall,
That standst betweene her fathers ground and mine,
Thou wall, ô wall, O sweete and louely wall,
Showe mee thy chinke, to blink through, with mine eyne,
Thankes curteous wall. *Ioue* shield thee well, for this.
But what see I ? No *Thisby* doe I see.
O wicked wall, through whome I see no blisse,
Curst be thy stones, for thus deceiuing mee,

    The. The wall mee thinkes, being sensible, should curse againe.

    Pyr. No, in truth Sir, he should not. *Deceiuing mee* is *Thisbyes* cue : she is to enter now, and I am to spy Her through the wall. You shall see it will fall

             H   Pat

1890
1900
1910
1920

1952
1960
1966-7
1970
1972
1980
1988

A Midſommer nightes dreame.

Pat as I told you : yonder ſhe comes.   *Enter Thiſby.*

Thiſ. O wall, full often haſt thou heard my mones,

For parting my faire *Pyramus*, and mee.

My cherry lips haue often kiſt thy ſtones;

Thy ſtones, with lime and hayire knit now againe.

Pyra. I ſee a voice : now wil! I to the chinke,

To ſpy and I can heare my *Thiſbyes* face. *Thyſby?*

Thiſ. My loue thou art, my loue I thinke.

Py. Thinke what thou wilt, I am thy louers Grace:

And, like *Limander*, am I truſty ſtill.

Thiſ. And I, like *Helen*, till the fates me kill.

Pyra. Not *Shafalus*, to *Procrus*, was ſo true.

Thiſ. As *Shafalus* to *Procrus*, I to you.

Pyr. O kiſſe mee, through the hole of this vilde wall.

Thiſ. I kiſſe the walles hole ; not your lips at all.

Pyr. Wilt thou, at *Ninnies* tombe, meete me ſtraight way?

Thy. Tide life, tyde death, I come without delay.

Wal. Thus haue I, *Wall*, my part diſcharged ſo;

And, being done, thus wall away doth goe.

Duk. Now is the Moon vſed between the two neighbors.

Deme. No remedy, my Lord, when wals are ſo wilfull, to heare without warning.

Dutch. This is the ſillieſt ſtuffe, that euer I heard.

Duke. The beſt, in this kinde, are but ſhadowes : and the worſt are no worſe, if imagination amend them.

Dutch. It muſt be your imagination, then; & not theirs.

Duke. If we imagine no worſe of them, then they of thēſelues, they may paſſe for excellent men. Here come two noble beaſts, in a man and a Lyon.

     Enter Lyon, *and* Moone-ſhine.

Lyon. You Ladies, you (whoſe gentle hearts do feare

The ſmalleſt monſtrous mouſe, that creepes on floore)

May now, perchance, both quake and tremble here,

When Lyon rough, in wildeſt rage, doth roare.

Then know that I, as *Snug* the Ioyner am

A

1930

1940

1950

2000

2005–6

2009
2010–11

2020

A Lyon fell, nor else no Lyons damme,
For, if I should, as Lyon, come in strife,
Into this place, 'twere pitty on my life.

Duk. A very gentle beast, and of a good conscience.

Deme. The very best at a beast, my Lord, that ere I saw.

Lyf. This Lyon is a very fox, for his valour.

Duk. True : and a goose for his discretion.

De. Not so my Lord, For his valour cannot carry his discretion : and the fox carries the goose.

Duk. His discretion, I am sure, cannot carry his valour,
For the goose carries not the fox. It is well : leaue it to his
discretion, and let vs listen to the Moone.

Moone. This lanthorne doth the horned moone present.

Deme. He should haue worne the hornes, on his head.

Duk. He is no crescent, and his hornes are inuisible, within the circumference.

Moone. This lanthorne doth the horned moone present,
My selfe, the man ith Moone, doe seeme to be.

Duke. This is the greatest errour of all the rest; the man
should be put into the lanthorne, How is it else the man ith
Moone?

Deme. He dares not come there, for the candle . For,
you see, it is already in snuffe.   (change.

Dutch. I am aweary of this Moone, Would hee woulde

Duke. It appeares, by his small light of discretion, that
hee is in the wane : but yet in curtesie, in all reason, wee
must stay the time.

Lysan. Proceede, Moone.

Moon. All that I haue to say, is to tell you, that the lanthorne is the Moone, I the man ith Moone, this thorne bush
my thorne bush, and this dogge my dogge.

Deme. Why? All these should be in the lanthorne : for all
these are in the Moone, But silence : here comes Thisby.

Enter Thisby.

Th. This is ould Ninies tumbe. Where is my loue? Lyon, Oh.

Demetrius

2066

Dem. Well roard, Lyon.

Duke. Well runne, *Thisby.*

Dutchesse. Well shone *Moone.* Truly, the Moone shines,
with a good grace.

2070

Duk. Well mouz'd, *Lyon.*

Dem. And then came *Pyramus.*

Lys. And so the Lyon vanisht.

Enter Pyramus.

Pyr. Sweete Moone, I thanke thee, for thy sunny beams.
I thanke thee, Moone, for shining now so bright.
For by thy gratious, golden, glittering beames,
I trust to take of truest *Thisby* sight.
But stay : ò spight! but marke, poore knight,
What dreadfull dole is here?

2080

Eyes do you see! How can it bee!
O dainty duck, o deare!
Thy mantle good, what, staind with blood?
Approach ye Furies fell,
O fates come, come, cut thread and thrumme,
Quaile, crush, conclude, and quell.

Duke. This passion, & the death of a deare friend would
goe neere to make a man looke sad.

Dutch. Beshrewe my heart, but I pitty the man.

Pyr. O, wherefore, Nature, didst thou Lyons frame?

2090

Since Lyon vilde hath here deflour'd my deare.
Which is, no, no : which was the fairest dame
That liu'd, that lou'd, that lik't, that look't with cheere.
Come teares, confound, out sword, and wound
The pappe of *Pyramus:*
I, that left pappe, where heart doth hoppe.
Thus dy I, thus, thus, thus.
Now am I dead, now am I fled, my soule is in the sky.
Tongue loose thy light, Moone take thy flight,
Now dy, dy, dy, dy, dy.

2100

Dem. No Die, but an ace for him. For he is but one.

Lys.

2000

2010

2020

Lyſ. Leſſe then an ace, man. For he is dead, he is nothing.

Duke. With the helpe of a Surgeon, he might yet recouer, and yet prooue an Aſſe.

Dut. How chance Moone-ſhine is gone before? *Thiſby* comes backe, and findes her louer.

Duk. Shee will finde him, by ſtarre-light. Here ſhee comes, and her paſſion ends the Play.

Dut. Me thinkes, ſhe ſhould not vſe a long one, for ſuch a *Pyramus* : I hope, ſhe will be briefe.

Demet. A moth will turne the ballance; which *Pyramus,* which *Thisby* is the better : he for a man ; God warnd vs : ſhe, for a woman; God bleſſe vs.

Lyſ. She hath ſpied him already, with thoſe ſweete eyes.

Deme. And thus ſhe meanes, *videlicet;*

This. A ſleepe my loue? What, dead my doue?

O *Pyramus,* ariſe,

Speake, ſpeake. Quite dumbe? Dead, dead? A tumbe

Muſt couer thy ſweete eyes.

Theſe lilly lippes, this cherry noſe,

Theſe yellow cowſlippe cheekes

Are gon, are gon : louers make mone :

His eyes were greene, as leekes.

O ſiſters three, come, come, to mee,

With hands as pale as milke,

Lay them in gore, ſince you haue ſhore

With ſheeres, his threede of ſilke.

Tongue, not a word : come truſty ſword,

Come blade, my breaſt imbrew:

And farewell friends : thus *Thyſby* ends:

Adieu, adieu, adieu.

Duke. Moone-ſhine and *Lyon* are left to bury the dead.

Deme. I, and *Wall* to.

Lyon. No, I aſſure you, the wall is downe, that parted their fathers. Will it pleaſe you, to ſee the Epilogue, or to heare a Bergomaske daunce, betweene two of our cõpany?

H 3   *Duke*

2030   2101–2   2106   2108   2110   2040   2113   +1   2050   2120   2130   2060   2136–7

Duke. No Epilogue, I pray you. For your Play needs no
excuſe. Neuer excuſe: For when the Players are all deade,
there neede none to be blamed. Mary, if hee that writ it,
had played *Pyramus,* and hangd himſelfe in *Thiſbies* gar-
ter, it wouldhaue beene a fine tragedy : and ſo it is truely,
and very notably diſcharg'd. But come your Burgomaske;
let your Epilogue alone.
The iron tongue of midnight hath tolde twelue.
Louers to bed, tis almoſt Fairy time.
I feare we ſhall outſleepe the comming morne,
As much as wee this night haue ouerwatcht.
This palpable groſſe Play hath well beguil'd
The heauie gate of night. Sweete friends, to bed.
A fortnight holde we this ſolemnitie,
In nightly Reuels, and new iollity.   *Exeunt.*
Enter Pucke.

Puck. Now the hungry Lyons roares.
And the wolfe beholds the Moone;
Whilſt the heauie ploughman ſnores,
All with weary taske foredoone.
Now the waſted brands doe glowe,
Whilſt the ſcriech-owle, ſcrieching lowd,
Puts the wretch, that lyes in woe,
In remembrance of a ſhrowde.
Now it is the time of night,
That the graues, all gaping wide,
Euery one lets forth his ſpright,
In the Churchway paths to glide.
And wee Fairies, that doe runne,
By the triple *Hecates* teame,
From the preſence of the Sunne,
Following darkeneſſe like a dreame,
Now are frollick: not a mouſe
Shall diſturbe this hallowed houſe.
I am ſent, with broome, before,

                                                To

To ſweepe the duſt, behinde the dore.

Enter King and Queene of Fairies, with all their traine.

Ob. Through the houſe giue glimmering light,
By the dead and drowſie fier,
Euery Elfe and Fairy ſpright,
Hop as light as birde from brier,
And this dittie after mee, Sing, and daunce it trippingly.

Tita. Firſt rehearſe your ſong by rote,
To each word a warbling note,
Hand in hand, with Fairy grace,
Will we ſing and bleſſe this place.

Ob. Now, vntill the breake of day,
Through this houſe, each Fairy ſtray.
To the beſt bride bed will wee:
Which by vs ſhall bleſſed be:
And the iſſue, there create,
Euer ſhall be fortunate:
So ſhall all the couples three
Euer true in louing be:
And the blots of natures hand
Shall not in their iſſue ſtand.
Neuer mole, hare-lippe, nor ſcarre,
Nor marke prodigious, ſuch as are
Deſpiſed in natiuitie,
Shall vpon their children be.
With this field deaw conſecrate,
Euery Fairy take his gate,
And each ſeuerall chamber bleſſe,
Through this palace, with ſweete peace,
Euer ſhall in ſafety reſt,
And the owner of it bleſt.
Trippe away : make no ſtay:
Meete me all, by breake of day. *Exeunt.*

Robin. If we ſhadowes haue offended,
Thinke but this (and all is mended)

H.4   That

63

A Midsommer nightes dreame.

That you haue but slumbred here,
While these visions did appeare.
And this weake and idle theame,
No more yielding but a dreame,
Gentles, dóe not reprehend.
If you pardon, wee will mend.
And, as I am an honest *Puck*,
If we haue vnearned luck,
Now to scape the Serpents tongue,
We will make amends, ere long:
Else, the *Puck* a lyer call.
So, good night vnto you all.
Giue me your hands, if we be friends:
And *Robin* shall restore amends,

FINIS.

2210

2220

2140

Signature	Page Number	Quarto Through Line Numbers	Riverside Edition
A2r	3	12–41	I.i.1–22
A2v	4	42–76	I.i.23–55
A3r	5	77–111	I.i.56–90
A3v	6	112–46	I.i.91–125
A4r	7	147–81	I.i.126–60
A4v	8	182–216	I.i.161–93
B1r	9	217–51	I.i.194–227
B1v	10	252–86	I.i.228–I.ii.10
B2r	11	287–321	I.ii.11–61
B2v	12	322–56	I.ii.61–100
B3r	13	357–91	I.ii.100–II.i.27
B3v	14	392–426	II.i.28–60
B4r	15	427–61	II.i.61–95
B4v	16	462–96	II.i.96–129
C1r	17	497–531	II.i.130–63
C1v	18	532–66	II.i.164–97
C2r	19	567–601	II.i.198–232
C2v	20	602–36	II.i.233–65
C3r	21	637–71	II.i.266–II.ii.30
C3v	22	672–706	II.ii.31–64
C4r	23	707–41	II.ii.65–97
C4v	24	742–76	II.ii.98–132
D1r	25	777–811	II.ii.133–III.i.12
D1v	26	812–46	III.i.12–52
D2r	27	847–81	III.i.53–89
D2v	28	882–915	III.i.90–126
D3r	29	916–50	III.i.127–62 S.D.
D3v	30	951–85	III.i.163–99
D4r	31	986–1020	III.i.200–III.ii.32
D4v	32	1021–55	III.ii.33–67
E1r	33	1056–90	III.ii.68–102
E1v	34	1091–1125	III.ii.103–35
E2r	35	1126–60	III.ii.136–70
E2v	36	1161–95	III.ii.171–203
E3r	37	1196–1230	III.ii.204–38
E3v	38	1231–65	III.ii.239–68
E4r	39	1266–1300	III.ii.269–301
E4v	40	1301–35	III.ii.302–32
F1r	41	1336–70	III.ii.333–65
F1v	42	1371–1405	III.ii.366–402
F2r	43	1406–40	III.ii.403–31

Signature	Page Number	Quarto Through Line Numbers	Riverside Edition
F2^v	44	1441–75	III.ii.432–IV.i.9
F3^r	45	1476–1510	IV.i.10–44
F3^v	46	1511–45	IV.i.45–78
F4^r	47	1546–80	IV.i.78–111
F4^v	48	1581–1615	IV.i.112–44
G1^r	49	1616–49	IV.i.145–78
G1^v	50	1650–83	IV.i.179–212
G2^r	51	1684–1715	IV.i.212–IV.ii.24
G2^v	52	1716–49	IV.ii.24–V.i.15
G3^r	53	1750–84	V.i.15–48
G3^v	54	1785–1819	V.i.49–83
G4^r	55	1820–54	V.i.84–117
G4^v	56	1855–89	V.i.118–51
H1^r	57	1890–1924	V.i.152–87
H1^v	58	1925–59	V.i.187–223
H2^r	59	1960–94	V.i.224–64
H2^v	60	1995–2029	V.i.265–307
H3^r	61	2030–64	V.i.308–54
H3^v	62	2065–99	V.i.355–89
H4^r	63	2100–34	V.i.390–424
H4^v	64	2135–48	V.i.425–438